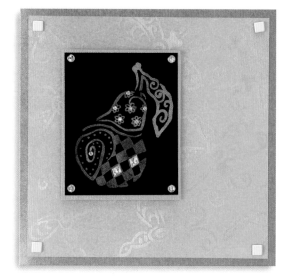

THE RUBBER STAMPER'S BIBLE

Françoise Read

David and Charles

HHA

A DAVID & CHARLES BOOK

David & Charles is a subsidiary of F+W (UK) Ltd.,
an F+W Publications Inc. company

First published in the UK in 2005

Distributed in North America
by F+W Publications, Inc.
4700 East Galbraith Road
Cincinnati, OH 45236
1-800-289-0963

A catalogue record for this book is available from the
British Library.

ISBN 0 7153 1850 0 hardback
ISBN 0 7153 1851 9 paperback

Printed in Singapore by KHL Printing Co Pte Ltd
for David & Charles
Brunel House   Newton Abbot   Devon

Commissioning Editor Fiona Eaton
Editor Jennifer Proverbs
Senior Designer Lisa Wyman
Production Controller Jen Campbell
Project Editor Jo Richardson

Visit our website at www.davidandcharles.co.uk

David & Charles books are available from all good
bookshops; alternatively you can contact our Orderline
on (0)1626 334555 or write to us at FREEPOST
EX2 110, David & Charles Direct, Newton Abbot,
TQ12 4ZZ (no stamp required UK mainland).

This book is dedicated to my mum and dad – Claudine and Don. Their love and support is second to none. I could not have completed this book without their constant encouragement and help. My love to you both.

Contents

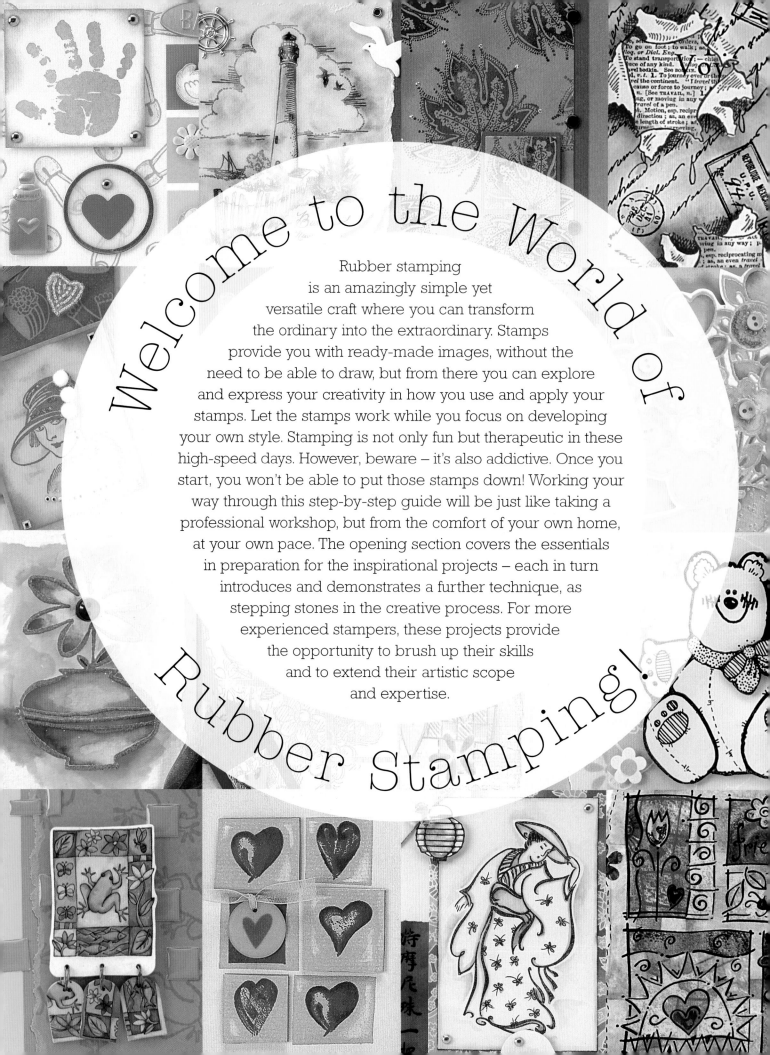

Welcome to the World of Rubber Stamping!

Rubber stamping is an amazingly simple yet versatile craft where you can transform the ordinary into the extraordinary. Stamps provide you with ready-made images, without the need to be able to draw, but from there you can explore and express your creativity in how you use and apply your stamps. Let the stamps work while you focus on developing your own style. Stamping is not only fun but therapeutic in these high-speed days. However, beware – it's also addictive. Once you start, you won't be able to put those stamps down! Working your way through this step-by-step guide will be just like taking a professional workshop, but from the comfort of your own home, at your own pace. The opening section covers the essentials in preparation for the inspirational projects – each in turn introduces and demonstrates a further technique, as stepping stones in the creative process. For more experienced stampers, these projects provide the opportunity to brush up their skills and to extend their artistic scope and expertise.

The Origins of Stamps

Rubber as a commodity has been around for hundreds of years. However, it was not until the process of vulcanization (hardening) was discovered by Charles Goodyear that a way ahead was found for a multitude of practical applications for rubber – stamps being one. Metal printing stamps preceded rubber varieties, and the actual source of the first rubber stamp is still a mired mystery. Early rubber stamps were marking devices such as those we still see in banks, post offices and libraries, and were mainly for commercial use, although the artist Pablo Picasso was partial to employing these stamps in his collages. The birth of modern rubber stamping, as we now know it, took place in the USA at the beginning of the 1980s, and with improved technology, we can now enjoy detailed, artistic designs.

How Do I Start?

If you are a beginner, work through the front section carefully and take time to select the right equipment, tools and materials, and to master the basic skills so that you have a sound foundation to build on, as well as the confidence with which to progress. If you have some stamping experience, this is a good opportunity to revisit the essentials, and you may well pick up some new tips to improve your skills. Besides practical techniques, this section looks at the fundamental principles of design involved in successful stamping – understanding and using colour, and composing and presenting images – with visual examples to show how these principles work in practice. You are then fully equipped to move on to your first project, adding a further technique to your repertoire, before progressing to the next. Each project is also accompanied by a gallery of additional designs featuring the key technique, which you can use as springboards for developing new ideas in your work. So, grab some scrap paper, pick up a stamp and inkpad and get stamping!

Why Choose Rubber Stamping?

It is no accident that rubber stamping is so universally popular, and its lasting appeal lies in the creative scope it offers and the variety of its applications. A stamp is like a tool, and once you master the basics of using it, it can be made to work in lots of exciting ways. Stamping can also be combined with other craft techniques, as demonstrated in the Creative Workshop – découpage, for instance – making it a multifaceted artistic endeavour with almost limitless creative potential.

Equipment

This section looks at the most essential, and specialist, equipment needed for stamping – stamps and inkpads. You may find the range and variety on offer confusing and overwhelming, but by following these simple, practical guidelines, you will be able to make the right choices according to what you want to achieve.

Stamps

There are many different kinds of stamp available, but they all fall into a few basic categories and are similarly constructed and used. However, there is a truy amazing range of images to choose from, covering every subject and theme imaginable.

Basic Construction

The most common type of stamp, a wood-mounted stamp, is made up of three components:

die This incorporates the image and is usually made from rubber. Always check that the image has a good depth to ensure a clear, clean print.

cushion This is made from foam and acts as padding between the block and the die. The cushion helps to distribute even pressure as you press down and raises the die.

block or mount This is the wooden handle to which the cushion and die are attached. You can see the stamp design, called the decal or index, on the block (see opposite).

Basic Design Types
Most stamps fall into one of two categories:

solid stamps The designs are made up of a solid rubber mass. Shadow stamps are a good example of a basic solid stamp (see page 46). Most of these stamps carry less detail, but interesting prints can be achieved by applying colour directly to the die with brush markers (see page 24).

outline stamps Prints made with these stamps produce the outline of an image that can then be coloured in (see page 62). On some of these stamps, shading in the way of dots or lines is part of the image (see page 74).

Varieties of Stamp

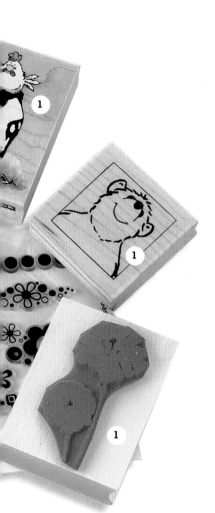

1 wood-mounted As we have seen opposite, these stamps consist of a rubber die on a wooden block. The decal or index is either attached as a label or is printed directly on the block. Some are coloured in as a guide to how they can be used, but always check the die against this printed image to see exactly what is going to be stamped. These are also available in themed sets.

2 foam-mounted These stamps usually come in sets and are cheaper to buy as the components are low-priced. Be careful not to print the corners of the stamps, as the dies are not trimmed.

3 clear These are made from polymer and the dies are self-clinging. Place them on a clear acrylic block to use (see page 22). Other types of clear stamps are available, but these are the simplest to use.

4 unmounted Some rubber dies are sold as separate items, either ones with foam that need to be mounted on a block or those that have to be stuck onto foam and cut out as well as mounted on a block. They are cheaper because you do the mounting and provide the block.

Stamp Images

There is a stamped image to suit every occasion you can possibly think of, from birthdays to Christmas, christenings to weddings and much, much more. Stamp sets are also available for these popular subjects and other themes, including alphabets for greetings and messages, so that you instantly have a range of co-ordinated images to use. As well as stamps with distinct motifs or images – and these include famous cartoon characters – there are large background stamps with all-over patterns for creating decorative backdrops. Stamps also come in different design styles, from contemporary to classical and period.

Start with one or two simple images, such as a flower or heart, which can have many applications. Further choices can be inspired by creating a card for a particular person.

Storing Your Stamps

✔ Store your stamps away from direct sunlight.

✔ To begin with, you may only need a single box to store your stamps. Pizza boxes, shoeboxes and photocopying paper boxes all work well as they have lids. If they are too deep, the sides can be trimmed down – two stamps deep is as far as you should go. Cut a blank piece of paper to fit in the bottom of the box. Arrange the stamps in the box and draw an outline of each wooden block, then make a print of each stamp in the appropriate space. Cover the printed sheet with plastic for protection.

✔ As your stamp collection grows, consider an office storage system or a specially designed unit for the storage of stamps. Some stampers prefer to set out their collection on narrow wall shelves for easy selection.

✔ To avoid duplicating images, keep a 'stamp log', where you stamp each new image that you buy.

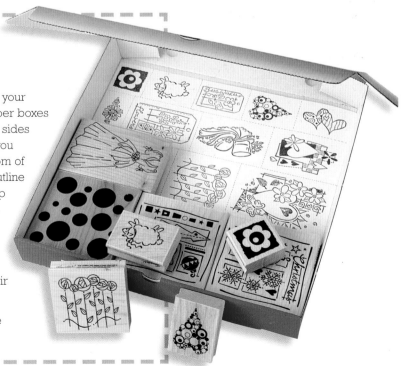

Inkpads

These come in a variety of sizes and shapes. Most inkpads have a raised sponge or felt pad, so that you can ink up a stamp of any size. Some inkpads come in single colours, while others are multicoloured.

When starting out on rubber stamping, with the wide range of different types of inkpad available, it is difficult to know which ones to select. Your choice should be largely dictated by the type of surface you are stamping on – see the table opposite for a guide to which of the leading brands of inkpad to use on different stamping materials.

However, all these inkpads fall into one of the following six main types of ink used for rubber stamping (see below).

1 multicoloured pigment inkpad

2 Vivid™ dye-based inkpads

3 Fabrico™ multipurpose craft inkpad

4 sponges – can be used for applying inks and paints to stamps

5 Re-inkers – these inks are available for most inkpads (see page 10)

6 Brilliance™ pigment inkpad

7 Dauber Duos™ – the smallest pigment inkpads available

8 Kaleidacolor™ dye-based inkpad

9 Cat's Eye® (due to its shape) pigment inkpad

10 square pigment inkpad

11 Clear Emboss™ inkpad

12 Ancient Page™ dye-based inkpad

13 Ancient Page™ small, shaped dye-based inkpad

14 Opalite™ pearlescent inkpad

15 Crafter's™ pigment inkpad

16 Vivid™ Premium Rainbow Dye inkpad

Dye-Based Inks

These inks are water-based, mainly non-permanent and usually come with a felt pad. They are available in a variety of colours, including multicoloured or 'rainbow' pads. Dye-based inks are translucent, dry quickly and can be stamped on most types of paper. However, images do appear brighter and crisper when stamped on white glossy paper.

Pigment Inks

These inks are thick, creamy and opaque, and usually come with a foam pad. They are available in a multitude of sizes and colours. Some colours are available in metallic, pearlescent and chalk finishes. Traditionally, most pigment inks are slow drying, but some have been developed to be faster drying, so it is important to check the label and ask for advice. The drying time will also depend on the weight and texture of the card you use.

Embossing Inks

These inks are usually clear or slightly tinted and most come with a foam pad. They are designed to dry slowly and to be used with opaque coloured and metallic embossing powders. If you like embossing, these inkpads are a useful addition (see pages 28 and 66). Embossing pens are also available that you can use to colour in and emboss a stamped image (see page 62). Some of these, known as dual embossing pens, have a different tip on either end, such as a brush, bullet or small and large chisel.

Resist Inks

These inks are formulated to resist or repel water-based dye inks on glossy paper (see Baby Bear, page 109). The VersaMark™ inkpad can be used to create a watermark or tone-on-tone effect in your stamping (see Frog Garden, page 101). It will also act as a 'glue' for chalks and paint powders (see pages 50 and 86).

Inkpad [trade name]	Type of Ink	Drying Rate	Permanent	Suitable Stamping Surfaces
Ancient Page™	dye	fast	yes, on absorbent surfaces	matt card, glossy card, vellum, style stones
Brilliance™	pigment	fairly fast	no, but it is stable enough to use with any wet colour medium when colouring in stamped images	matt card, glossy card, vellum, shrink plastic, acetate, clay, leather, wood
ColorBox Fluid Chalk™	pigment	fast	yes, if heat set	matt card, glossy card, style stones
ColorBox Pigment Ink™	pigment	slow	no, but embossing will make it suitable to use with any wet colour medium	matt card [glossy card, vellum, wood and acetate with embossing only]
Crafter's™	pigment	slow	yes, if heat set	matt card, fabric, shrink plastic, wood, style stones
Dauber Duos™	pigment	slow	no, but embossing will make it suitable to use with any wet colour medium	matt card [glossy card, vellum, wood and acetate with embossing only]
Emboss™ (Clear or Tinted)	pigment	slow	no, since its primary use is for embossing	matt card
Encore™	pigment	fairly slow	no, but embossing will make it suitable to use with watercolour mediums	matt card [vellum with embossing only]
Kaleidacolor™	dye	fast	no	matt card, glossy card
Perfect Medium™	pigment	fairly slow	no, since its primary use is for the application of Perfect Pearls™	matt card
StazOn™	solvent	fast	yes, no heat setting necessary; use in a well-ventilated area	vellum, shrink plastic, acetate, glass, acrylic, metal foil
VersaColor™	pigment	slow	no, but embossing will make it suitable to use with any wet colour medium	matt card [glossy card, vellum, wood and acetate with embossing only]
VersaMark™	resist	fairly slow	no	matt card, glossy card [as a resist]
Vivid™	dye	fast	no	matt card, glossy card

Fabric/Craft Inks

Although some fabric inks are manufactured primarily for use on fabric, types such as Fabrico™ and Crafter's™ are multipurpose craft inks that can also be used on wood, leather, shrink plastic and unglazed ceramics (see page 114). When stamping on fabric, heat setting is required and fabrics should be pre-washed to remove sizing (see page 19).

Permanent/Solvent Inks

Permanent inks are available in both water- and solvent-based forms and can be used on most types of card as well as other surfaces such as wood, acetate, shrink plastic, glass, metal foil, leather and acrylic. Most are ideal for non-porous and semi-porous surfaces. You may need a special stamp cleaner to remove solvent inks from your stamps, and these inks should always be used in a well-ventilated area.

Inkpad User's Guide

All the inkpads listed in this chart are used in the techniques pages and projects in the book. Re-inkers are also available for all these inks so that you can refresh the pads if they dry out. There are many more inkpads available, but these will give you an excellent range to build on.

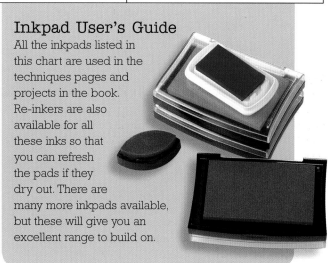

Making Them Last

You can greatly increase the lifespan of both inkpads and rubber stamps if they are properly looked after. Keep them in tip-top condition, and you'll always have your favourite stamps and colours to hand.

Re-Inking Your Inkpads

Never throw away dry inkpads. Re-inkers are available for most inkpads – small bottles of ink that you can use to bring your inkpads back to life. Always try to re-ink your inkpads as evenly as possible.

1 Squeeze the bottle gently to apply the ink evenly over the entire surface of the inkpad.

2 Use a piece of thick card or an old plastic card to drag any ink still on the surface of the inkpad across until it has been soaked up.

workshop secret

Only dye-based inkpads, which have a felt rather than a sponge pad, need to be stored upside down, so that the ink travels to the pad surface and doesn't dry out. If multicoloured inkpads are stored upside down, they must be kept level.

Cleaning Your Stamps

If you care for your stamps properly, they will last you a lifetime. Try to clean your stamps straight away after use. At this stage, most inks can be cleaned off using water. However, for some inks, such as solvent inks, you need to use a specific stamp cleaner. Avoid as much as possible wetting the wooden mount when removing the ink. This could affect the adhesive used to stick the die and cushion to the wooden mount. The following are some stamp-cleaning options.

water
Take a shallow tray or an old plastic lid. Fold up several layers of kitchen roll, place them in your container and wet with water. Dab your stamp onto the wet kitchen roll.

baby or wet wipes
These are handy for cleaning stamps, but make sure they are alcohol- and lint-free. Alcohol will dry out the rubber die, while lint will leave hairs behind after cleaning.

brushing
If you have ink in the recesses of your stamp that will not come away, use a soft toothbrush to scrub away the residue. You can also use a Magic Carpet™, which is like a rectangle of thin, open-pile carpet. As the stamp is pushed against its surface, the tips of the pile clean the recesses.

Tools

When starting a craft, it is difficult to decide which tools are necessary and which ones can be acquired at a later stage. So, begin by checking out the items in the Basic Tool Kit – you may find that you already have some of these at home. All the tools listed in the kit are used throughout the book, so make sure you have these to hand.

Basic Tool Kit

scissors • paper trimmer • craft knife • self-healing cutting mat • ruler • bone folder • pencil • pencil sharpener • eraser • paintbrushes • heat gun

Scissors

Good-quality, sharp scissors are essential for cutting out stamped images. Keep one pair purely for paper cutting and they will stay sharper for longer. Small nail scissors, straight and curved, are useful for cutting out very intricate designs.

Paper Trimmer

Several models are available – choose one with a replaceable blade that can cut down a sheet of A4 (or US letter) card. If you are likely to be making a large amount of cards, it may be worth investing in a professional guillotine.

Craft Knife and Self-Healing Cutting Mat

A craft knife is useful for trimming card and cutting out intricate designs. Disposable blades are best, as they become blunt with use (keep the blade safely covered when not in use). A craft knife should always be used with a self-healing cutting mat. These come in all sizes, but A4 (or US letter) is the most useful. Most are printed with a grid and measurements to help with cutting and trimming. Keep it clean and never use it with a heat gun – the intense heat will make it warp.

Ruler

A transparent plastic ruler is ideal when measuring and marking. A metal ruler should be used when trimming card with a craft knife, otherwise it will cut into and damage the edge of a plastic ruler. A long ruler is useful for large pieces of card.

Bone Folder

Manufactured cards come pre-scored, but a bone folder is invaluable if you want to score and fold cards yourself, helping you to achieve crisp, neat folds (see page 40).

Pencil, Sharpener and Eraser

Use an ordinary lead pencil for marking measurements on card and paper. A hard pencil (2H) makes light, easy-to-erase marks. A sharp point is most accurate when measuring and marking, so use a good-quality sharpener (one with a cover will keep your workspace tidy). Make sure your eraser does not smudge as opposed to rubbing out, and is clean before use.

Paintbrushes

If you enjoy painting in your stamped images, a selection of different-sized paintbrushes is a must. Quality is important, but good nylon brushes are available at a reasonable price. Never leave your brushes standing in water for too long to avoid damaging the tips.

Heat Gun

Although mainly used to melt embossing powders (see page 28), this does have further applications. It can be used to dry work in progress (see page 21), to heat set certain inks (see page 115) and to heat shrink plastic (see page 99). It must be used with care and work surfaces should be protected from the intense heat. Store it away from young children.

Creative Tools

Once your stamping progresses, you will feel more confident and may need to extend your kit. So here is a list of further useful tools. Most of these you can see in use in the individual projects in the Creative Workshop.

Fancy-Edged Scissors

Use these to cut fancy borders or edges (see Christmas Nativity, page 97). Scalloped and deckle-edged are just two of the types available. Other popular designs include Victorian and postage stamp.

Punches

Choose from the many shapes and sizes to create embellishments for your work, such as hearts, flower heads and stars (see page 44), or decorative corners and borders (see page 95). Keep them sharp by occasionally punching them through kitchen foil. Punch aids are available if you find it difficult to apply the required pressure.

Single Hole Punches

These come in a variety of sizes, but 1/8in and 1/16in are the most useful. Use them to make holes for brads (paper fasteners), snaps (poppers), eyelets, wire and ribbon (see pages 64 and 84). An 'anywhere' hole punch is useful when you have to make holes away from the card edge, where you cannot reach with an ordinary hole punch (see page 52).

Tweezers

Tweezers are useful for lifting and holding tiny and delicate items such as gems and beads or peel-off stickers, or for pulling ribbon, threads and wire through punched holes.

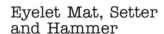

Eyelet Mat, Setter and Hammer

Eyelets are used for attaching stamped panels to the base card and for finishing the holes in tags, but they also act as a versatile embellishment. To fix eyelets in place, after punching the correct size hole for the eyelet with a hole punch (see left), you need an eyelet setter and a hammer (see Step 9, page 112, for the eyelet fixing technique). To protect your work surface, work over a special eyelet mat or use an old telephone directory. Snaps (poppers) are used and fixed in the same way (see page 116).

Wire Cutters and Round-Nose Pliers

If you plan to use wire in your work, you will need proper wire cutters for cutting medium and thick wire (see page 64). The thickness of wire is referred to as the gauge, and the higher the number gauge, the thinner the wire. Wire cutters can also be used for cutting metal foil (see page 102) and mesh. Round-nose pliers are useful for bending and holding the wire.

Sponges and Daubers

These can be used to apply inks to backgrounds and stamped images (see pages 54 and 63). Different kinds of sponge will achieve a variety of textures, for instance, a natural sponge will produce an open texture. Rounded sponges ensure a more even effect, without any visible lines. Sponge Daubers™ are designed to fit on your index finger, keeping your hand clean.

Stipplers

These apply tiny dots of colour to fill a stamped image or create a background (see page 87). Different types are available, but they achieve a similar, subtly textured effect. They can be used to blend colours and produce graduated tones.

Glue Dispensers

Depending on the model, these dispense either a line of glue or tiny glue spots or glue tabs. These make gluing a clean and easy process.

Paint Palette

An old plastic lid or CD case will serve as a makeshift palette, but if you don't want the colours to mix, then a proper palette with individual wells is the solution. It is also helpful for mixing up powder-type paints such as Perfect Pearls™ or Pearl-Ex™ (see page 15) to create your own colour palette.

Brayer

This paint roller-type tool is great for creating backgrounds (see page 106) or for inking up large stamps (see page 21). One that has a detachable roller is more useful.

Xyron™ Machines

These apply glue evenly onto the back of items, such as ribbon, punched shapes, pressed flowers and vellum, rolled through the machine. Different sizes are available for tiny to larger pieces. Replacement cartridges are available.

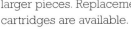

Dry Embossing Tool and Foam Mat

A dry embossing tool can be used to score card (see page 40), for frosting or dry embossing vellum (see page 82) and for indenting or embossing metal foil (see page 102). Use one with a large ball for working on vellum, while a dual tool with a medium and fine ball on either end is useful for other purposes – the fine ball is best for scoring. When using on vellum, you need to work over a surface that will give, such as a piece of fun foam or a computer mouse mat.

Stamp Positioner

This is a special stamping tool that enables you to stamp precise patterns, borders and frames. If you need to stamp an image or wording in a very specific place, a stamp positioner makes it easier to achieve (see page 25).

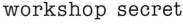

---

workshop secret

When you have accumulated a range of tools for rubber stamping, look for a suitable storage container to keep them all together, preferably with separate compartments for easy organization and access – DIY stores offer a wide range to choose from. Portable storage is particularly useful if you don't have a dedicated workspace or for when you are stamping away from home.

Materials

Once you have acquired a few stamps, inkpads and some basic tools, you will need a range of materials to help you construct your stamped work into cards and to add to the finish. Making the right choice of these materials, depending on the purpose, will ensure that the results of your efforts are as professional as possible.

Adhesives

A single adhesive will not cover all your needs in stamping, where different types of glue are required for mounting card and paper and for adhering embellishments to card. The following is a guide to the main types of adhesive, which are used in many of the projects in the Creative Workshop. In addition, a reel of ordinary adhesive tape is a must. Xyron™ machines and glue dispensers are also very handy (see page 13).

Spray Glue

Spray glue is useful for sticking larger pieces of card or paper. The permanent form of spray glue offers excellent bonding qualities, but the re-positional form is also very useful. Always use a spray glue in a well-ventilated area on a large, covered surface.

PVA Glue

This type of glue has a strong bond and dries clear. Choose a good-quality variety – Hi-Tack Glue™ is particularly good, since it is flexible, so is perfect for sticking embellishments to cards, such as bows and buttons. Make sure you have a supply of cocktail sticks and cotton buds for applying the glue to small items.

Sticky Fixers

These adhesive foam pads are used specifically in 3-D découpage (see page 78), but they are also widely used to attach elements to a design so that they are raised from the surface. They are available in a variety of thicknesses.

Clear Adhesive Dots

These easy-to-use dots come on a paper strip, which is simply pressed face down onto the required area. Available in a variety of sizes – down to miniature dots – it is important to choose the right size for the work you are doing. They also come in different thicknesses, the thicker ones being useful for raising elements from the background surface.

Glue Stick

This is useful for sticking small items, such as punched shapes, and using on thin card, but it isn't suitable for use on large items because it is brittle and may lift if the card bows.

Foil Adhesive

This is used for applying foil to stamped images (see page 43). It is available in different forms, including as a pen, which is handy for applying the glue to particular areas of an image or for lettering. The thin glue must be allowed to dry until it is tacky before the foil is pressed onto it.

Double-Sided Tape

This resembles ordinary adhesive tape, but it is sticky on both sides. Once a piece or strip has been stuck in place, the backing is removed to reveal the other adhesive side. This is a firm favourite with stampers, since it is easy and clean to use.

Decorative Materials

There is a huge range of these to choose from to add colour, textural and dimensional interest to your stamped designs.

Colouring Mediums

Pencils, chalks, paints, brush markers and felt-tip pens are the main colouring mediums used in stamping. Experiment to find the ones that you feel most comfortable using. However, each of these mediums can be used to create different effects (see Colour Effects, pages 33–35).

Embossing Powders

These are heated and melted to create a raised outline or surface on stamped images. See pages 28–30 for more information about embossing powders and the essential techniques.

Dimensional Magic™

As its name indicates, this product adds dimension to images as well as highlights. It dries clear and creates a dome-like casing over the area to which it has been applied.

Glitter

Glitter usually comes loose or pre-mixed with glue in small bottles (see page 111 and She Sells Sea Shells, page 45). Available in a phenomenally wide range of colours, some are opaque, while others are transparent. The finer the glitter, the better the quality and coverage.

Liquid Pearl™ and Liquid Appliqué™

Both of these products have come to stamping via fabric painting, and they are available in a range of colours and applied straight from the bottle. Liquid Pearl™ is best for adding little dots of pearlescent colour or small highlights to stamped images (see Pink angel, page 85). Liquid Appliqué™ is used in conjunction with a heat gun, the heat causing it to raise and puff up. It is ideal for snowmen or animal designs, but can also be used generally to add dimension and texture.

Pearlescent Paint Powders

Powder paints such as Perfect Pearls™ and Pearl-Ex™ can be dusted over a still-wet stamped image or mixed with water to create a paint medium (see page 86). Pearl-Ex™ is also available in a palette as a pre-mixed, ready-to-use paint.

Peel-Off Stickers

These mostly outline stickers, available in gold, black and silver and a range of other colours, offer useful finishing details for stamped designs, such as 'faux' brads and eyelets, frames and borders, letters and Chinese characters, as well as motifs, such as butterflies (see pages 60, 86 and 102). They also come in holographic form (see Ornate Trees and Golden Pear, page 89).

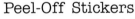

workshop secret

You may find a craft knife helpful for lifting small peel-off stickers from their backing sheet and accurately positioning them on your design.

Surfaces

Just about anything can be stamped once its surface is smooth and if the appropriate ink is used. It is easier if the surface is flat, but it is possible, with practice, to stamp on curved surfaces, such as on terracotta flowerpots or thick candles. If you are starting out in rubber stamping, card and paper are the easiest and most popular surfaces to stamp.

Card and Paper

Such an abundance of choice exists in terms of colour, texture, finish, weight and size that no two cards need ever look the same! The type of card and paper you use will partly dictate your choice of ink. Most card and paper is machine made and the quality does vary greatly, so check carefully when buying your stock. Some types of white card can look almost grey and this will dull the colours you use. Certain kinds of coloured card can fade very quickly. For a professional look, choose quality over quantity. Handmade papers are very popular and they can be useful to add a unique touch to a finished card. Heavily textured papers are not suitable for stamping, but can be used for layering and mounting.

Card
These are some of the most popular and versatile types of card used by stampers, although there are many more besides.

matt
Although available in many colours and varying thicknesses, white and cream are the two most popular colours used by stampers for stamping on and to use as folded cards. The surface is smooth and has good absorbency. It will also cope with a range of colouring mediums.

linen
Mainly available in white and cream, the surface mimics that of linen fabric. The texture is very subtle, making it suitable to stamp on if it is not coated with a finish.

hammered
The surface resembles that of sheet metal that has been hammered, with lots of tiny bumps. Usually available in white and cream, it is used mainly for folded cards.

pearlescent and metallic
These are suitable for both stamping and folded cards. Special inks such as Brilliance™ (see page 9) need to be used, as the surface does not always absorb the ink sufficiently well. Always test the ink on a small area to check suitability before you begin a project.

watercolour
This is the best type of card to use with paint or ink mediums that need water to spread the colour over the surface. It is able to absorb lots of water very easily, but be aware that it will do the same with the ink you use to stamp it with. It comes in a variety of weights (thicknesses) and textures from smooth to rough. It is best to use the lightest weight and least textured for stamping.

Making the Right Choice

When choosing card or paper for stamping, you need to consider the following points:

✔ **Ink** What type of ink can you use on this card or paper?

✔ **Absorbency** How long does the ink take to dry on the card or paper? Will it dry at all or will it need to be embossed? Is the ink drying too fast to be embossed (see pages 28–30)?

✔ **Density** Is it difficult to tear? Is it flexible or does it crease easily?

✔ **Finish** Is the card glossy, coated, metallic, pearlescent or matt?

✔ **Texture** Is the card smooth and flat? How difficult would it be to stamp on?

✔ **Weight** Is it thick enough to make into a folded card? Is it more suitable for layering?

✔ **Acid-free and archival** Is it suitable for a piece of work that you want to preserve?

shaped and aperture cards

As well as rectangular- and square-shaped folded cards, cards are available ready-cut into particular shapes, such as handbags, shirts, shoes and fans. These can add a further fun dimension to your work. Others have pre-cut apertures – square/ rectangular or round/oval – that are ideal for framing a stamped image.

corrugated and perforated

Corrugated card is thinner and more refined than the packing material, and comes in many colours. Although not suitable to stamp on, it is great for layering and for folded cards. Some cards are patterned with perforations or holes, which again are suitable for layering and the holes can be used for threading ribbon and yarn or for attaching buttons with thread.

Papers

Again, these are some of the basic types of paper out of the many available that offer stampers a good range of applications and effects.

background papers

The choice here is phenomenal. There are plain and patterned, and most come in collections, which means you can mix and match colours and designs easily. They are used mainly as backgrounds and for layering. They are ideal for covering a plain card or for collage elements. Most are suitable to stamp on.

vellum

This looks very much like tracing paper and shares some of its qualities. It comes in a range of colours and thicknesses; some are printed with patterns, have metal flecks imbedded or a shimmering surface, while others are embossed. Vellum is great for layering and is easy to stamp on with the right ink (see page 9). You can dry emboss the surface yourself to achieve a frosted effect (see page 82).

velvet

This coated paper looks and feels just like velvet fabric. You can stamp and emboss on it with stunning results, and use colouring pencils to highlight the stamped images. You can even press a pattern into the surface (see page 95). It is also good for layering and punching.

glittered

This is paper coated with a layer of thin glitter, which makes it unsuitable for stamping but great for layering.

foiled

On these striking papers, the pattern has been applied with foil that resembles shiny metal. They are more suitable for layering than for stamping.

pearlescent and metallic

Papers as well as card are available in both these finishes. Being that much thinner, the papers are best used for stamping and layering rather than for folded cards. Purchase them in strips for punching and small card work.

duo

These have a different colour on each side, sometimes two tones of the same colour, for easy co-ordination. If you intend combining paper cutting and folding techniques, such as Lacé®, in your work, these papers will offer you a greater colour choice.

giftwrapping

Some of these papers may be suitable for stamping, while others make excellent background papers.

Storing Card and Paper

✔ Always store your card and paper flat, away from direct sunlight and in a dry environment.

✔ Organize them for easy access, so that you can clearly see what you have available and avoid damaging the corners by searching through sheets. Keep offcuts for punching out.

✔ If you begin to work on a few cards at a time, find somewhere safe to store them. Some card suppliers manufacture clear plastic wallets to fit their blank cards, which are ideal. These are also great if you want to sell your cards.

Other Creative Surfaces

Once you have gained in skill and confidence in stamping on card and paper, experiment with the variety of other mediums and extend your creative repertoire. As you can see from the projects featured in the book, it is easy and fun. Other surfaces that can be used for stamping include cork, mountboard or extra-thick card, polymer clay or modelling compound, wood, fabric, leather, glass and ceramics.

Shrink Plastic

Available in translucent and opaque white, clear, cream and black sheets, shrink plastic can be stamped, coloured, cut out and baked to make items such as jewellery, badges, fridge magnets, buttons and miniature panels (see page 98). It sometimes comes pre-sanded on one side. If not, you will need to sand it before stamping with an extra-fine grade paper wrapped around a sanding block using a circular motion, to give the ink a texture on which to key. Several manufacturers produce shrink plastic, so check the individual product's instructions.

Style Stones

These are inkable, cultured stones that come in two finishes, coated and natural. The coated stones are ivory in colour and have flat surfaces that are ideal for precise stamping and colour blending. The natural stones are white in colour and have engraved surfaces. These are ideal for simple stamped designs and colouring. Both can be used to embellish cards or to create jewellery pieces. They come in a variety of shapes including tags, frames and hearts (see page 114).

Acetate

Acetate is a thin, transparent plastic that comes in sheets ready to use (see page 110). Not all acetate is heat resistant, so check or experiment before using a heat gun to emboss or set the ink. Not all permanent inks need to be heat set – use a StazOn™ inkpad if in doubt (see page 9). Acetate allows you to layer stamped images on top of each other.

Metal

Tin metals or thin sheets of metal foil are suitable to stamp on (see page 102). The surfaces of tin metals can be sponged with ink before stamping. You can also change the colour of real copper by heating it with a naked flame. Metal foil comes in a variety of colours and its surface can be drawn into to create additional texture.

Cork

A few manufacturers produce extra-thin, smooth sheets of cork, ideal for stamping. Most inks and other colouring mediums can be used on its surface. It is easy to cut with scissors or a cutter, but it can also be torn to give a very effective edging.

Mountboard and Mini Matts™

Both mountboard and Mini Matts™ are manufactured from layered card. This makes them very strong and they are less likely to warp with the application of paint and embossing powders than ordinary card. Mini Matts™ come pre-cut in a variety of shapes, such as hearts, triangles and frames. Mountboard is normally used for picture frame mounts, so offcuts are easy to purchase from framing shops.

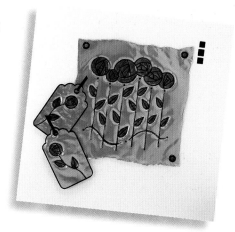

Leather

Choose leather with a smooth surface for stamping, avoiding embossed or heavily textured varieties. Use fabric or craft inks to stamp. Start with a simple item such as a belt. You can also stamp chamois leather, but it must not be heated or ironed, otherwise it will shrink.

Fabrics

Smooth weaves, such as muslin, silk, cotton sheeting and cotton T-shirts, will give you the best stamping results. Before stamping, always wash a fabric to remove the sizing and prevent any further shrinkage once the design has been stamped. In addition to clothing, other fun items such as canvas shoes and bags can be stamped.

Polymer Clay or Modelling Compound

Fimo™ and Sculpey™ are just two types of polymer clay that can be stamped. They are easy to use and can be baked in an ordinary oven. The clay should be rolled out smoothly so that the image can be stamped evenly. Use polymer clay to create stamp-embellished jewellery, such as earrings and brooches. If you enjoy working with clay, a pasta machine and shaped cutters would be useful additions to your tool kit.

Wood

Wood can be unfinished (untreated and bare) or finished (varnished and sealed). Extra care should be taken when stamping unfinished wood – the surface is easier to stamp if it has been sanded down to a smooth finish and partly sealed to stop the ink bleeding. A good range of unfinished wood items is available from craft stores such as boxes, trays and simple shapes.

Ceramics

Glazed ceramic surfaces require much the same treatment as glass surfaces. Some ceramic items are available unglazed, making them easier to stamp and colour in, such as porcelain tiles, shapes and coasters. Unglazed ceramics, unlike glass (see below), can be embossed, but they can only be used for decorative purposes and will not withstand being washed and cleaned.

Glass

Due to the popularity of glass painting, a variety of glass objects are available from craft stores that are suitable for stamping. The very smooth surface of glass makes it a little more difficult to stamp, so start with the simple shapes on offer, such as hearts, circles and ovals. Stamping works best for purely decorative items, since they require little handling and washing that would damage the design. Do not stamp and decorate eating or drinking surfaces. Never emboss glass, as the intense heat from the heat gun could shatter the glass.

workshop secret

If you are stamping on glass, wipe the surface with methylated spirits beforehand to remove any grease or other residues that might cause the ink to resist, then handle as carefully as possible to avoid leaving fingerprints on the surface.

Stamping Workshop

In this practical workshop, you are guided through the stamping process, stage by stage, so that you are fully equipped with the essential skills as well as the confidence to begin stamping in earnest. After perfecting the art of inking and printing, including advice on how to use clear stamps, we look at other basic techniques such as colouring stamps with brush markers, how to position your stamps accurately, masking and embossing.

Basic Stamping

Although you can be shown how to ink up a stamp and make a print, nothing beats hands-on experience. With practice, you will develop a feel for how much ink to use and the amount of pressure you must apply to achieve a good print.

Applying Ink to Stamps

The first stage of stamping, once you have chosen a stamp, an appropriate inkpad and card or other stamping surface, is to apply the ink to the stamp. This must be done in the right way to ensure a strong, clean print. The surface of the rubber on new solid stamps can sometimes be reluctant to hold the ink, leading to patchy stamping. If so, you may need to use and clean the stamp several times to remove any manufacturing residue that is preventing the ink keying onto the surface (see page 10).

Before You Begin

- ✔ Always stamp on a flat surface.
- ✔ Cover your work surface with scrap paper. This keeps your workspace clean and gives you a place to experiment with the stamps and ink before you start.
- ✔ Make sure any stamp you use is clean and dry.
- ✔ Check the condition of the inkpad for wetness and remove any unwanted bits of fluff or other debris.

small stamps
If a stamp is considerably smaller than the inkpad you are using, you can tap it directly onto the surface of the pad.

1 Place the stamp on a flat surface, rubber-side up. Tap the inkpad gently against the surface of the rubber to apply the ink. Do not press the inkpad against the rubber or too much ink may be released onto the surface.

2 Hold the stamp up to the light and the wet ink should glisten. You should be able to see if you have missed any areas or if the ink has been applied evenly.

over-inking
This is how a stamp looks if it has been over-inked. There should be no ink in the recesses, on the rubber around the image or on the wooden block. Try not to waste ink in this way.

using a brayer

A brayer makes it easier to apply an even coat of ink to stamps, especially large stamps. Holding the inkpad firmly with your spare hand, roll the brayer back and forth over the inkpad, letting the roller spin around when it comes off the pad, so that the whole roller is evenly covered in ink. Then roll back and forth over the surface of the stamp until evenly covered with ink. Re-ink the brayer as necessary.

using multicoloured inkpads

Always ink up the stamp so that the colour bands run in the same direction. Try not to go over complete colour bands or the inks on your inkpad will mix. This could ruin the inkpad, especially if the colours contrast greatly or go from light to dark. Alternatively, use a brayer.

inking specific areas

Use small inkpads to apply different-coloured inks to specific areas of a stamp. Always start by applying the lightest colour first.

Making a Print

Have lots of scrap paper ready and practise your printing technique until you get the right results.

inking open areas

When a stamp has large, open areas, use the edge of the inkpad to tap over the outside of the stamp rather than directly over the top. This will stop ink gathering in the open areas, but if it does, clean the ink away with a cotton bud before stamping. However, it is preferable to use a small inkpad for inking up these types of stamps, rather than the large kind shown here.

1 Grip the wooden mount of the stamp on either side with your fingers. Press it, rubber-side down, on the card using firm, even, downward pressure. Try not to rock the stamp. The larger the stamp, the more pressure you need to apply.

2 Gently lift up the stamp away from the card and check the printed image left on the surface.

3 Let the print dry naturally before handling. To quicken the process, use a heat gun (see page 28). If you do not have one to hand, lay a piece of clean scrap paper over the stamped image, hold it in place with one hand and gently press the paper down over the image with the other, to blot off the excess ink.

Using Clear Stamps

Clear stamps are becoming increasingly popular – they are very easy to use, take up very little storage space and are good value for money. The dies are generally made from a transparent polymer that you mount onto a clear acrylic block to create a stamp that you can see through! This enables you to stamp with great precision. In addition, they allow you to combine different elements or images and colours with ease, so that you can compose and create your own individual designs.

Preparing the Stamp

The clear dies come as a set, stored between two plastic sheets. One of the sheets is printed with the designs contained within the set. This is the storage base to which you should always return the dies. The other plastic sheet covers and protects the dies.

1 Lift the die you want to use from the plastic sheet with your fingers. The dies are self-clinging and may require a little gentle tugging to remove.

2 Place the die on a clear acrylic block that is larger than the die itself. No part of the die should extend beyond the block to avoid an uneven print.

Making a Print

1 Ink up the die and stamp on the card. You can see exactly where you are stamping and what pressure you are applying by looking directly through the clear acylic block.

2 Remove the die, clean it and replace on the sheet. Select and ink up the next die. Hover over the card to decide where the next image needs to go and stamp. Remove and clean the die.

3 Ink up the final die you need to complete the image. As you can see through the block and die, it is easy to apply several colours precisely.

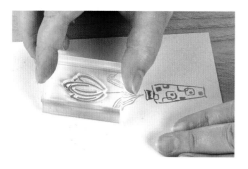

4 Stamp the final part of the image. Having separate dies for individual sections of an image allows you to create a multicoloured design relatively easily.

5 Rather than stamping the image in individual sections, arrange the dies on a larger block if you want to compose a whole image before stamping.

workshop secret

If you are using a tiny die and only have a large acrylic block, you can balance the block by placing an additional uninked die in the opposite corner to the die you are printing with.

varying the designs

As the polymer is flexible, some dies can be mounted on the block in different ways. For instance, a border or word can be arranged so that it is curved or wavy rather than straight.

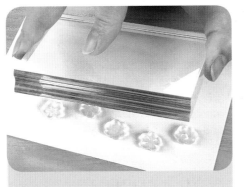

pre-arranging dies

Sometimes it is easier to arrange the loose dies on your work surface prior to mounting them on the block. Make sure they are facing the right way, stamping-side down. Lower the block over the top carefully and press down to secure the dies in place. This technique is helpful when you need to compose a special wording from individual letters.

precision placement

If you want to be precise in how you mount the dies on the block, you can draw guidelines on the block with an OHP (overhead-projector) pen, which can later be removed, if necessary, with an acohol-based cleaner. Use a different colour for each set and a flexible ruler for curved lines.

Caring for Clear Stamps

✔ Always clean the dies and blocks straight away. Wash the dies in soapy water, using a small bowl for small dies to avoid losing them down the plug hole. This will also revive their clinging power. You can use other household cleaners for the blocks, but avoid anything abrasive that might scratch the surface. A solvent cleaner will remove any colouring medium, including chalk, which is otherwise difficult to shift.

✔ Store your clear stamps in a plastic wallet. Remember that the dies are self-clinging, so keep plastic items away from uncovered dies.

Having Trouble with Printing?

Whatever the type of stamp you are using, if you are not satisfied with your printing efforts, analyse the results of your printing and see whether you are making one (or more!) of these common mistakes:

A If the print is uneven in weight, with areas missing, you are applying insufficient and uneven pressure.

B If the print is over-heavy and blurred, you are applying too much pressure, too much ink and/or rocking the stamp.

C If black smudges appear in open areas of the stamp, you have failed to clean up excess ink from these areas before stamping.

Brush Markers

The simplest way to make a print without an inkpad is to use brush markers or felt-tip pens. You simply draw with the tip of the pen directly onto the rubber die of the stamp. As the colouring of the image is completed before it has been stamped, you can apply lots of different colours to one image. This technique works equally well with solid or open designs. It is very quick to master and the results are instant.

Part Inking

With some designs, using brush markers enables you to stamp only part of the image.

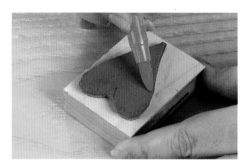

1 Place your stamp, rubber-side up, on the work surface. Hold in place while you colour in the surface of the die with the brush markers, lightest colour first.

2 Apply the next colour, making sure to overlap the first colour very slightly so that you do not leave patchy gaps. Continue until the entire die is covered.

1 Select the area of the stamp you want to use and apply colour to it.

3 Hold the stamp up towards your mouth to huff (not blow) air over the die. Some brush markers dry quickly, so the moisture from your breath revives the inks.

4 Stamp your image straight away after reviving the inks.

2 Huff on the die and stamp the image. With this stamp, you can use the hearts individually.

Fading Out

Fading out is a useful technique for grouping single images such as trees, balloons, leaves or butterflies and can be achieved with inkpads as well as brush markers.

1 Apply the colours to the die, starting with the lightest colours first. Apply two shades of each colour to create depth.

2 Huff on the die and carefully stamp the image.

3 Do not apply any further colour to the die, but simply huff over the die again and make a second print, which will be lighter. Overlapping each print will add depth to the arrangement.

Accurate Positioning

When you need to stamp an image in a specific place or to stamp a precise pattern, a stamp positioner will act as a guide so that you can position and stamp your image accurately (see page 13). It is a useful tool for both beginners and advanced stampers. Practise using the tool with a suitable stamp on some scrap paper and card.

1 Line up the corner of a thin, see-through sheet of paper with the inside corner of the stamp positioner. Always check that the paper you are using is exactly square.

2 Hold the positioner in place with one hand while you stamp the image in the corner of the paper. Try to guide and locate the mount of the stamp squarely in the corner of the positioner.

3 Position the stamped image on the paper over the card so that it is exactly where you would want to stamp it.

4 Carefully line up the inside corner of the positioner with the corner of the stamped paper.

5 Remove the stamped paper, but leave the stamp positioner and card in place. Repeat the process from Step 2 onwards to stamp the image on the card. The image should be exactly positioned on the card.

6 Repeat the lining-up process to stamp the next part of the design precisely in position on the card.

7 Once you have finished stamping your design, you can trim down the card. Without a positioner, this frame would have been very difficult to stamp sufficiently accurately.

Masking

Masking, meaning to cover or hide in stamping, is mainly used to print images overlapping one another, so that one appears to be behind the other. It can also be used to stamp an image within a frame or to sponge a background. It is a useful technique and the results are great fun.

Cutting a Mask and Grouping Single Images

To create a group of a single image, a mask of the image is used to cover the main image while it is being stamped with overlapping prints of the same image, so that it remains in the foreground.

1 Stamp the image on the front of the stick-on notepad over the adhesive band of the pad that is on the back. Use permanent ink, so that it will not bleed when it is stamped over.

2 Using small, sharp scissors, cut out the image, cutting just slightly into the outline. This will prevent a halo effect when you stamp over the edge of the mask. If you are using a thicker paper, you will need to cut away more.

Choosing Paper for Masks

Any paper can be used to make a mask, but the thinner it is, the better. Stick-on notes are ideal because they are thin, removable and reusable. They come in a variety of sizes and are also inexpensive. Masking films made specifically for rubber stamping can be found in craft shops.

4 Make sure that the first image is dry before placing the mask over the top – the sticky part on the back should hold it in place. Stamp the second image partly over the mask to create the illusion of depth.

3 Stamp the main, forefront image onto the paper first.

5 Keep the mask in place if you want to stamp more overlapping images.

workshop secret

Having taken time to stamp and cut out a mask, place it on a plastic or paper sheet and store away in a plastic wallet or file for future use.

Creating a Sponged Background

By using a cutout mask to protect a central stamped image and masking off an area around the image, a subtly textured coloured background can be quickly created with sponged-on ink.

workshop secret

If your image is much larger than the example shown, construct a frame to fit by laying strips of paper around the image; use a set square to ensure that the corners are exact right angles. The strips could be torn for added interest.

1 Stamp and cut out the mask. Stamp the image on the card and cover with the mask. Punch a large square in a stick-on note and discard the square but keep the frame. Place the frame over the stamped image. Add further stick-on notes around the frame for protection. Sponge ink over the mask and edges of the frame.

2 When sponging is complete, lift off the mask and frame. Colour in the stamped image.

Stamping Within a Frame

Rather than having to position and fit a stamped image within a frame, a mask of the frame can be cut to protect the stamped frame so that another image can be stamped across and overlapping the aperture. Once removed, the second stamped image is contained within the frame.

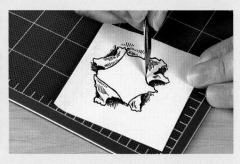

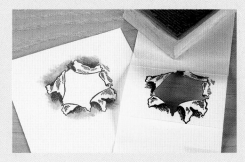

1 Stamp the image on the stick-on note. Using a sharp craft knife and working over a cutting mat, cut around the inside outline of the image to create a frame.

2 Stamp the image on the card and colour in.

3 Place the mask over the stamped image, adding further stick-on notes for protection. Stamp an image over the aperture, removing the mask when the ink has dried.

4 A mask can be created to cover the aperture so that a further image can be stamped around it to create a background.

Simple Embossing

Embossing is the 'wow' factor in stamping, giving stamped images a raised line or surface. It is achieved in three stages – first the image is stamped, then an embossing powder is applied and finally the image is heated. The heat melts the particles of the embossing powder together so that they form a plastic skin. This is an easy technique to learn and one that will extend the creative use of your stamps. You can emboss onto many different surfaces including card, paper, heatproof acetate, wood, metal foil and fabric.

Embossing Powders

These come in a variety of types that basically fall into the following categories:
- metallic and coloured (opaque)
- pearlescent (semi-transparent)
- glitter or sparkly (opaque, semi-transparent or clear)
- clear (transparent).

Most stampers start off with gold and silver. Always check the label to find out which type the powder is so that you can choose the appropriate inkpad for stamping.

If the powder is opaque, you can use a Clear or Tinted Emboss™ or VersaMark™ inkpad, or coloured pigment inkpad – it is useful to match this to the colour of the embossing powder.

If the powder is semi-transparent or clear, consider which colour pigment or embossing inkpad it will be applied to.

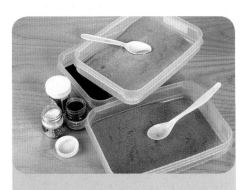

storing powders

If you use some powders on a regular basis, it is worth storing them in shallow containers with lids, with a spoon inside ready for use.

reducing static

Before stamping, wipe the card with an anti-static puff to greatly reduce the risk of excess powder sticking to the card. Not only does it combat static, but it helps counteract any moisture, which some cards absorb more than others.

Using a Heat Gun

✔ There are several different models of heat gun on the market, so try to see them in action to select the right one for you.

✔ It is possible to use an empty toaster for heat embossing by holding your work with a peg over the top, image-side up, until the powder melts. However a proper heat gun is much safer and more reliable.

✘ Do not use a hair dryer, as it blows out too much air and the heat is not sufficiently intense to melt the powder.

✔ Always protect your work surface from the intense heat. An old chopping board or piece of mountboard is good.

✘ Never work over a cutting mat, as it will end up warped!

workshop secret

To save excess powder, fold the paper used to catch the excess powder in half to create a funnel. Pour the powder back into the jar.

1 Stamp your image on white card using a Clear or Tinted Emboss™ inkpad – a tinted inkpad will make it easier for you to see where you have stamped the image.

2 Sprinkle the embossing powder carefully over the image. Apply just enough powder to cover the image. You may find it easier to sprinkle the powder with a spoon.

3 Gently shake off the excess powder from the stamped image onto a clean piece of paper and put aside. The wetness of the ink will hold the powder in place over the stamped image. Check for any areas that you may have missed.

4 Place the stamped image on a suitable surface and heat the powder. Hold the heat gun at least 2.5cm (1in) away from the surface and move it around from one area to the next as the powder melts. Work in good light so that you can see the image changing as the powder melts. Once the whole image has risen and turned shiny, stop heating. If you over-heat the image, it will sink into the card and appear oily.

Ink and Embossing Powder Combinations

It can sometimes be useful to stamp an image using the same colour that will be used for embossing, especially if you miss any areas in the embossing process. Gold on gold works well, but try these other combinations for different effects.

For a stronger colour
• copper embossing powder over brown ink
• black embossing powder over black ink

For a softer colour
• pearlescent blue embossing powder over black ink
• pearlescent gold embossing powder over gold ink

5 Once embossed, the image can be coloured using felt-tip pens, colouring pencils or paints (see pages 33–35). The raised outline makes it easier to keep the colouring medium within the outline of the image.

Resist Embossing

Resist embossing mimics the traditional art of batik, in which a resist is created on fabric with wax. Here, the resist is achieved with embossing powder. This technque is useful for creating co-ordinating backgrounds over which other stamped elements can be layered. With practice, several colours can be blended to create striking backdrops.

1 Ink up the background stamp with a Clear Emboss™ inkpad. With large background stamps, it is best to turn the stamp on its back on the table top and dab the inkpad over the stamp. Check that the stamp is fully covered with ink by holding it up to the light and seeing if the whole surface of the rubber glistens.

2 Place the background card directly on the surface of the inked stamp. Using the fingers of one hand, gently rub and press down on the back of the card. At the same time, keep the card in position with your other hand.

3 Sprinkle clear embossing powder over the stamped card and shake off the excess. Using a heat gun, heat the powder until melted – apply the heat gun systematically to avoid missing any sections, which is easy to do when heat embossing large areas.

4 When the card has cooled, using a Sponge Dauber™ to pick up ink from a pigment inkpad, apply ink all over the embossed card. Be generous with the layer of ink to achieve a good coverage.

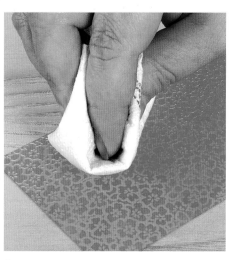

5 Gently rub a pad of kitchen roll all over the card to remove any unwanted ink from the embossed areas. As the excess ink is removed, the pattern created by the stamping and embossing will become clearer. The embossed areas now resume the colour of the card.

Colour Workshop

There is a wealth of colour choice and opportunities on offer to stampers for every element used in their craft, from card and paper, stamping inks and embossing powders, to all the different mediums for colouring in and highlighting stamped images, as well as embellishments, such as ribbon, beads and stickers. Facing this range of options can be bewildering, and deciding what to use and in what combinations for the best results rather daunting.

However, armed with some basic principles on choosing and using colour, and some practical pointers on all-important pre-planning, you will quickly gain confidence and find the task creatively rewarding.

Where to Start

❀ Take inspiration from the stamp designs you are thinking of using.

❀ Consider the person for whom you are creating your design, their personality, likes and dislikes. For instance, what colour clothes do they wear or what style of home decor do they favour? Are they extrovert or relatively quiet? Are they animal or nature lovers, or do they have a particular pastime that they love, such as sailing or shopping?

❀ If your design is to mark a special event, such as a birthday or wedding, bear in mind that colours reflect mood, so bold, bright colours are good for birthdays, while pastel palettes are appropriate for weddings, in keeping with the soft, romantic theme.

❀ Choose a theme that naturally has colour associations. In an African theme, for example, the colours will be rich and warm browns and earth tones. Cool blues and greens are suitable for water and nature themes.

❀ Collecting materials you wish to feature in your designs can prompt a colour scheme. For instance, a piece of ribbon or patterned paper can be enough to inspire a palette or suggest a link between colours.

Sources of Inspiration

❀ Purchase a professional colour wheel from an arts and crafts shop.

❀ Look around you for colour schemes that work effectively in furnishings, clothes or household items.

❀ Collect paint swatch strips from a DIY store that you can place together to see how the colours work together. These strips are particularly useful to see how a colour tone will change as it becomes either lighter or darker.

Getting Colour-Wise

✔ There is often a stamped line or outline to an image, and this should also be considered as part of your colour scheme. Choosing black, white, gold or silver for stamping your outlines will each react with and affect the colours they surround in a different way, changing their intensity. For instance, black will enhance the vibrancy of bright colours, while a lighter colour will complement pastel colours.

✔ Add further interest to a colour scheme by applying it in a variety of textures and finishes.

✔ Work on two identical cards at the same time and use one to try out colours or shading. When colouring in your designs, always select your pencils or pens before starting and test to see if the colours work together first.

Understanding Colour

Intensity refers to the brightness or dullness of a colour. The intensity of the colours that you choose for your stamped designs will obviously change the appearance of your work. Here are some simple colour schemes with visual samples.

Bright

Use red, yellow, blue, green, orange and purple at their strongest intensity to create a bright, cheerful scheme that will be ideal for fun children's cards or for a contemporary design featuring summer flowers or butterflies.

Pastel

Mix a colour heavily with white and it will look soft and light. Baby cards and wedding cards are favourites for this colour scheme.

Blacks, Whites and Neutrals

Black sets off colours, while white softens a colour's intensity. Blacks and whites look great with most other neutral colours, including browns and greys. This colour scheme lends itself to vintage designs or old-fashioned images, and is particularly useful for men's cards.

Monochromatic

This is one of the easiest colour schemes to work with, in which you use varying shades of just one colour – you cannot go wrong! Pick a colour that is suitable for your subject and get stamping.

Achromatic

This colour scheme, often referred to as colourless, uses only blacks, whites and greys. It is a useful approach for a modern look or for etched-like images.

Cool and Warm

Blues, greens, purples and pinks are regarded as cool colours, and are effective in combination, while yellows, oranges, reds and browns are considered warm. Think about these colour ranges in terms of how they occur and work in nature, where they have obvious warm or cold associations, such as sunsets for warm, and sea and woodland for cool.

Complementary

For maximum impact and intensity, select complementary colours. These colours work in pairs – red and green, orange and blue, and purple and yellow. A Christmas design is a perfect application for the classic reds and greens combination.

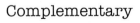

Colour Effects

Once you can stamp, it is fun and rewarding to spend time adding colour to your creations. There are lots of different mediums to choose from. To begin, you may already have some at home that you can experiment with, such as colouring pencils or felt-tip pens. Others you may be able to see being demonstrated in shops or at craft shows. It is amazing how each medium can change the look of a stamped image, thus giving you extra options for your stamps. It is important to try different mediums and find ones that you feel confident to use and that give you the look you want to achieve.

1 pre-mixed pearlescent paints

2 watercolour pencils

3 watercolour felt-tip pens

4 decorating chalks

5 foil palette with inkpad colours

6 soft-leaded colouring pencils

7 waterbrush and colour sketch brushes

8 fine-nib felt-tip pens

9 brush markers

10 permanent pens

11 watercolour paints in tubes

12 multipurpose craft inks, and Fantastix™ brush and bullet-tip applicators

Watercolour Effects

Watercolour enables you to build up layers or washes of colour, to blend colours for a range of subtle tones and to shade an image to add a sense of depth. Always stamp with permanent ink or emboss, otherwise the outlines of the stamped images could bleed.

Brush Markers

1 Stamp an image ready to colour. Using the brush markers, apply a little of each colour you want to use onto a plastic palette or an old plastic lid.

2 Dip a clean paintbrush into some water. Use the wet brush to dilute the colour on the palette. If the colour in the palette has already dried up, the water will activate it and make it usable.

3 Start to apply colour to the stamped image. Always begin with a very pale wash that you can gradually intensify. Continue to add colour until the desired shading is achieved. Keeping the colour darker around the edge of an area helps to create a three-dimensional effect.

Watercolour Felt-Tip Pens

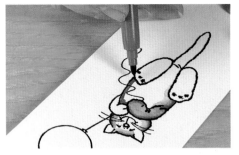

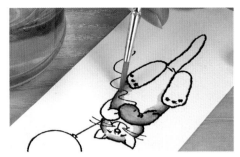

1 Use a watercolour felt-tip pen to colour in the outer edge of one area at a time of the design.

2 Dip a clean brush into some water and paint over the colour applied with the pen. This will activate the colour and at this stage you can drag some of the colour out from the edge to wash it over the open areas of the image.

Watercolour Pencils

1 Colour only small sections of the stamped image with the watercolour pencils. Consider which areas should be light or dark. Colour in the dark areas.

2 Dip a clean brush into some water and paint over one colour at a time to activate it. Drag out some of the colour into the open areas.

3 Alternatively, you may find it easier to use a waterbrush. This is a brush that has a water reservoir. Unscrew the brush end and fill the reservoir with water by holding the handle slightly under the water level and squeezing.

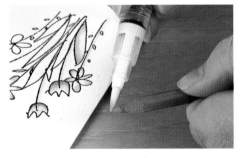

4 You can also pick up colour directly from a watercolour pencil with a wet paintbrush or waterbrush to paint your stamped image.

pearlescent paints
Dip a clean brush into some water. Apply the wet brush to the surface of the pearlescent paint to activate it and pick up the colour.

Pearlescent and Metallic Effects

These mediums create quite a contrast in effect to what we have seen before. Pearlescent paints make a bold impact, especially when used on dark card, such as black as in this example. The paints can be mixed and blended together to create further colours. A less intense effect yet still with a luxurious sheen can be produced with metallic pencils.

metallic pencils
These again work well on dark backgrounds, which accentuate the metallic finish. Pencils are easier to handle and apply than paints, especially if you are just getting started with colouring.

Colouring Effects in Comparison

It is worth experimenting with the range of techniques shown to compare the results of using different mediums to colour the same stamped image. These samples show at a glance what a variety of effects can be simply and effectively achieved.

A ordinary felt-tip pens, used straight from the pen

B ordinary felt-tip pens, colour picked up from a palette and mixed with water (see Brush Markers, page 33)

C colouring pencils, shaded and blended

D decorating chalks, image stamped in brown for a softer look

Chalk Effects

Try easy-to-use decorating chalks for a softer look, especially suitable for delicate subjects such as flowers, or for cute, cuddly images such as teddy bears or mice. These come in a palette form with a choice of 9 or 24 ready-to-use colours and can be used with any type of inkpad. All you need to apply them is small pieces of cotton wool and cotton buds. A chalk enhancer will add depth and intensity to the colours. Turn to the project on page 50 to learn more about using chalks in different ways.

1 Stamp your chosen image – for an even softer look, stamp in a colour other than black, such as the brown used here. Start applying chalks to the larger areas of the design using pieces of cotton wool, applying the lightest colour first. Simply rub the surface of the chalk block with a little cotton wool to pick up the colour.

2 Use a cotton bud to fill in the smaller areas and to add detail. Use one cotton bud per colour.

3 A special chalk enhancer liquid can be applied with a cotton bud or other applicator over the colours to intensify or blend the chalks. Watercolour-type effects can be achieved or the enhancer can be mixed directly with the chalks before they are applied.

Embellishments

Embellishments not only offer another form of colour, but provide the decorative detail and final finishing touches for your stamped designs. The selection available from craft shops and suppliers is amazing, making it is easy to find just the right items to personalize your cards, complement your main designs or simply to express your individual creativity. However, also take a close look at the materials you may already have at home with a fresh eye to their creative potential, such as old buttons, broken jewellery and postage stamps, and keep on the lookout for interesting elements to incorporate in your future designs. Start collecting now!

1 eyelets

2 snaps (poppers)

3 brads (paper fasteners)

4 charms

5 buttons

6 beads

7 micro beads

8 seed beads

9 Fun Flock™

10 metal shapes

11 glitter glue

12 foils

13 ribbon

14 yarns

15 silk tassels

16 small reels of wire

17 large reel of wire

see-through storage

There are lots of handy storage items available to keep your embellishments where you can find them and in good order. Separate small, transparent stacking boxes or a flat box with separate compartments are ideal for sorting beads, buttons or eyelets by colour or shape, and you can see exactly what you have at a glance, for easy selection.

brads (paper fasteners), snaps (poppers) and eyelets

These are useful for attaching materials to cards that are difficult to glue, such as vellum, foil and acetate, and other elements such as tags and charms, but they can also be purely decorative (see pages 50, 110 and 114). They all come in a range of sizes, shapes and colours. Brads simply require a hole punched in the card, through which the two prongs are pushed, then bent outwards to flatten on the back of the card. To fix eyelets and snaps in place, you also need an eyelet mat, setter and hammer (see pages 12 and Step 9, page 112).

beads, buttons and charms

These come in an endless variety of colours, shapes, textures, finishes and sizes. They can be sewn on directly or threaded onto wire, ribbon or yarn (see pages 66 and 90). If you want to glue them on, you must use a PVA glue that has the requisite flexibility, such as Hi-Tack Glue™.

fun flock™

This is made from shredded felt and is useful as a coating, creating a soft, textural effect. Use it to mimic animal fur or snow on a snowman. First colour in the area you want to cover, apply a thin layer of liquid glue, then a matching colour of Fun Flock™, pressing it onto the glue.

micro beads

These are tiny beads without a hole. They are used mainly as a coating to decorate or highlight part of an image.

natural embellishments

Shells, skeleton leaves, feathers and pressed flowers are all available from craft shops, so there is no need to plunder the beach or garden. They are a useful addition for popular outdoor themes such as gardening and fishing. Small shells are great when combined with seed beads for a beach scene (see She Sells Sea Shells, page 45).

glitter glue

This is a liquid glue that contains glitter and comes in a wide range of rich colours. It is great for adding sparkling highlights to images, and is useful for creating a waterdrop effect.

flat-backed acrylic gems and diamond dots™

Any item that sparkles is useful when it comes to embellishing cards. Flat-backed gems come in a range of colours and shapes including stars, hearts, tear drops, triangles, squares and dots (see page 80). Those that come on strips are self-adhesive; loose gems have to be glued. Diamond Dots™ are flat, self-adhesive shapes backed with glitter (see Wedding Bells, page 85, and page 111). Snowflakes and flowers are effective, but many other shapes are available. Cover a Diamond Dot™ with a drop of clear glue for a dimensional, dome-like effect.

foils

Available in single sheets or small rolls in a variety of plain colours, these add a touch of luxury to any card. Multicoloured foils are also available in an amazing range of patterns and colours. You can use foil to fill in whole images or simply to highlight small areas such as the tips of butterfly wings or flower petals (see page 43). You will need a special foil glue to stick the foil in place (see page 14).

ribbon, yarns, raffia and string

Ribbon comes in a wide variety of materials, textures, patterns, colours and widths. The theme of the card will often dictate your choice of ribbon type, be it sheer, silk or paper (see pages 58 and 74). Use it to add bows or to tie around a card with a knot. If you want a less formal or more natural look, raffia or string is the ideal solution (see Sail Away, page 53, and page 70). Yarns can offer vivid colours and fun textures, and look great tied to tags (see page 54). You can also make your own tassels from yarns, or use ready-made silk tassels for a more sophisticated design.

wire

Thin wire can be used like a thread and is great for attaching beads to cards. Have fun twisting wire around sticks to make springs (see page 64) or have a go at making miniature coat hangers or paper clips. Besides standard-sized reels, sets of small reels of decorative wire are available in a good selection of colours.

Presentation Workshop

Good presentation is vital if you want your stamping to look professional, and the self-satisfaction that comes with producing the right results is a reward in itself. First you need to consider some basic design principles that will help you to compose images, select colours and add embellishments to best effect. Just as important in presentation is to know how to make a basic folded card so that it is a perfect foundation on which you can build your design.

Square Cards

Square cards, with their even dimensions, lend themselves to symmetrical, more formally composed designs. The precise centre of the card provides a strong focal point. Square motifs understandably always work well on a square card, but a more upright-shaped image can be combined with another element alongside – a tag or other embellishment – to create an overall square-shaped design.

❮ A small stamped image is given maximum impact by being placed exactly in the centre of the card.

❮ The image is layered, each layer varying in colour and width to create contrast. The same motif is used for the background.

❮ You can use an odd number of images on a square card by mounting them vertically in a row to one side or down the centre.

❮ This design lacks a focus of interest, as the four repeated images are set too far apart on the card.

❮ The four repeated images have been grouped in the centre of the card and now work together to give a focus to the design.

❮ To take the four-image composition further, the images are mounted on a panel, which provides them with a frame.

One stamp – five card designs!

This sequence shows you how the same stamped image can be presented in different ways to create a variety of designs. This has been achieved by simple changes to the layering of elements and by adding a few basic embellishments. All the cards are produced using a standard A6 or 14.8 x 10.5cm (or 5½ x 4¼in) card (see Before you Begin – Card Sizes/Formats, page 40).

❮ Borders play an important role in presentation. Used to frame and enhance an image, they can be built up in several layers of the same width, for a stepped effect, or you can combine small and large borders, as in this example.

❮ Only a very narrow border of the white card is left showing, but this is enough to work with the white edge of the torn panel. The large purple panel has been stamped with a subtle all-over pattern to create a textural effect.

Tall Cards

As with square cards, it is a failsafe approach to choose a tall-shaped image to fit on a tall card, and this will add dramatic emphasis to the image, making it appear even taller. The dynamic dimensions of tall cards lend them to asymmetrical designs. Tall cards are also perfect for repeating a simple motif, either exactly in line or at varying angles, to create a vertical linear design. Remember too that a tall card can be turned on its side to make a long, landscape-shaped card – ideal for featuring a row of stamped images.

 ❬ With the stamped image positioned centrally on a tall card, the design looks strangely awkward and unharmonious.

 ❬ The image is mounted towards the top of the tall card, where the eye will naturally focus, and so the design now works.

 ❬ The image is layered on pieces of card, with each layer varying in colour and the edges trimmed in a different way to create contrast and further interest. The addition of a vertical row of tiny punched hearts takes the presentation a step further.

 ❬ The three images are set too far apart and evenly on the card, and so the design lacks focus and interest.

 ❬ Grouping the three images together and positioning them towards the top of the card achieves focus and visual balance.

 ❬ The three images are layered on contrasting card, cut into strips rather than the usual panels, and varying in width and in the way they are trimmed for extra visual interest. The addition of a couple of tiny punched hearts takes the presentation a step further.

 ❬ Background panels do not have to be rectangular or square. Two tags varying in size have been layered and used to display the stamped panel.

 ❬ For added interest, two edges of the stamped panel have been torn at an angle. The brads can be placed away from the corners for a variation on the composition.

 ❭ The same image has been repeated to form a row to create quite a different look and an alternative landscape-format card. The torn edges of the purple border layer complement those of the main panel.

Making a Folded Card

Now that you have seen how the basic design principles work in practice and taken inspiration from these presentation ideas, all you need to do is take a little time to learn how to make a perfect folded card, then you can start experimenting with stamping designs and projects.

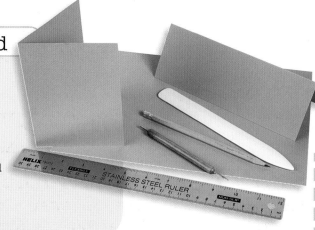

You Will Need

- ✿ paper trimmer or craft knife and cutting mat
- ✿ metal ruler
- ✿ hard (2H) pencil
- ✿ dual dry embossing tool
- ✿ eraser
- ✿ bone folder

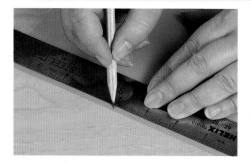

1 Using a paper trimmer or a craft knife and a metal ruler and working over a cutting mat, cut the card down to the required size, making sure it is precisely square – use a set square to check that the corners are right angles if necessary. With the card wrong-side up, measure and mark the halfway point along the top and bottom of the card with a hard (2H) pencil. Double check this measurement before you move onto Step 2.

2 Place the ruler on the card aligned with the two pencil marks. Use the fine ball on the dry embossing tool to score a line against the ruler. Go over the line a couple of times to make sure that the score has indented the top layer of card. If you under-score, the card will not fold neatly; if you over-score, the fold will be too loose. Rub out the pencil marks. If you are using a paper trimmer, it may have a scoring blade that you can use.

3 Fold the card so that the scored line is on the inside. Press the card together gently.

4 The card can be creased and folded by hand, but for a neater finish, it is best to run the flat edge of a bone folder over the fold. Make sure that the bone folder is clean or cover the card with thin paper or tissue to protect it.

Before You Begin

✔ **card sizes/formats**
A lot of card is sold in packs of A4 (or US letter) sheets. It is useful to know that if you cut it in half widthways, you can create two A6 or 14.8 x 10.5cm (or 5½ x 4¼ in) cards from one sheet. You can also score and fold one or both halves lengthways to make a tall or long card.

✔ **check the grain**
Before cutting, check the direction of the grain. Bend the sheet horizontally and vertically without creasing – it will flex easily with the grain. When the card is folded with the grain, it will bend quite easily and the fold will have a clean edge; if folded against the grain, it will be difficult to fold and the crease will be rough and broken.

✔ **check the right side**
Some cards will have a definite right side, while with others it will be a matter of personal preference. With linen cards, the more textured side is the right side. Score on the wrong side of the card.

Creative Workshop

Découpage • Shadow Stamping • Chalks • Sponged Backgrounds • Bleaching Out
Embossing Pens • Multi Embossing • Masking • Cut Away • 3-D Découpage
Vellum • Pearlescent Effects • Collage • Velvet Paper • Shrink Plastic
Metal Foil • Brayering • Acetate • Style Stones

Découpage

You Will Need

- ❀ 3 different sheets of co-ordinating patterned paper
- ❀ white folded card 21 x 8cm (8¼ x 3¼ in)
- ❀ lilac and fuchsia pearlescent papers
- ❀ graphite black Brilliance™ inkpad
- ❀ butterfly stamp
- ❀ foil
- ❀ foil glue pen
- ❀ flower punches
- ❀ peel-off stickers: black brads

top tip

Use simple, graphic stamps with a bold outline that are easy to cut out. With experience, you can tackle more intricate designs.

Découpage is the craft of cutting out printed images and gluing them onto a flat surface. Stamped images are ideal, and stamping onto patterned papers is a clever way of filling the stamped outline.

Shimmering foil highlights the wings of the pretty butterflies, and the finished look is so flat that it looks pre-printed!

1 Prepare the patterned papers for the background of the card. Cut a piece of the first sheet of patterned paper to cover half the front of the tall white folded card and stick in place with spray glue. Tear a strip of the second patterned paper and stick it to the other side of the card, overlapping the edge of the first.

2 Using the black inkpad, stamp three butterflies down the middle of the card. Ensure that the images lie across both the patterned papers and change the angle of the stamp each time to help create the impression of fluttering butterflies.

3 On the third sheet of patterned paper, stamp three more butterflies using the black inkpad. Enclose interesting patterns within the stamped shape, such as bold marks and colours – these areas will become the wings of the butterflies on the finished card.

4 Using small, sharp scissors, cut out the wings and body of the three butterflies, leaving behind the antennae (you will not need these). Always cut through the middle of the black outline to ensure that none of the background paper colour will show up on the finished card.

5 Use foil to create sparkly highlights on the tips of the butterfly wings. To do this, apply foil glue to the tips of the wings with a foil glue pen. Allow the foil glue to dry clear and then gently press the foil, shiny-side down, onto the glue. The glue will pick up the foil as you peel it away.

try this
Glitter could be used instead of foil to create an alternative highlight. Either use a glitter glue or apply a thin coating of PVA glue and then sprinkle on loose glitter.

6 Using a glue stick, position and stick the butterflies that you have cut out and foiled directly over the ones stamped on the folded card, aligning them with the antennae already there.

7 Punch out flowers of different sizes from the pearlescent papers. Create a couple of double flowers by sticking a small flower on top of a medium one. Arrange all the flowers on the card before sticking them in place with a glue stick.

top tip

Use a glue stick for gluing paper pieces accurately into position, as this type of glue allows for some movement and positioning time.

SMART STAMPING

Découpage

✔ Use thin papers to avoid building up bulky layers.

✔ Select the pattern carefully – avoid large patterns for small images and vice versa.

✔ Work with papers from one collection in a project, since mixing designs can be difficult to co-ordinate.

✔ Plan how you want the pattern to lie within the stamped outline, as this can enhance or lessen the effect of movement.

8 Place a brad in the centre of each flower. Use a craft knife to lift off the brads from their backing sheet and to position them accurately on each flower.

More ideas for découpage

Leafy Tag

A large tag makes a perfect quick card or special bookmark. The brown and green printed papers were chosen to work with the leaf stamp. The leaves within the square were simple and easy to cut out. Additional images were then stamped, cut out and découpaged onto the main image. Brads and eyelets, plus a hand-drawn stitched border, were added to enhance the card. The tag was finished with a selection of interesting wool and fibres, which could be threaded with beads.

Sunny Hello

This intricate design was created using five different patterned papers from the same collection to build up the découpage layers. The image was stamped five times on each paper, then the pieces cut out, assembled and glued over the image stamped once on the base blue paper. Two to three layers were built up in each boxed section for a three-dimensional feel. Foil was applied to highlight the flowers and hearts, and a hand-drawn stitched line added for a home-spun, patchwork finish.

She Sells Sea Shells

With an ever-expanding range of printed papers now available, why not create themed découpage cards? Background papers featuring seahorses, shells and starfish prints co-ordinate perfectly with the marine stamps. The folded card was covered with the paper using spray glue to achieve a strong bond and flat surface. To continue the seaside theme, a raffia bow was added and small, real shells (widely available from craft stores) embellish the card. Glitter glue adds a final sparkle to the shells, as if the waves had just washed over them.

Shadow Stamping

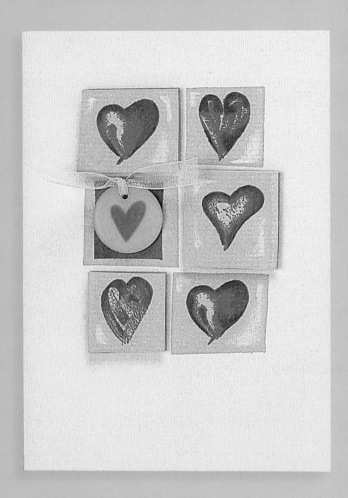

You Will Need

- ❀ pink folded card 14.5 x 10.5cm (5¾ x 4¼ in)
- ❀ pink card
- ❀ orchid pastel and dark peony ColorBox Fluid Chalk™ inkpads
- ❀ set of 6 irregular background blocks, small single open block and heart stamps
- ❀ dark purple and white soft-leaded colouring pencils
- ❀ narrow pink sheer ribbon
- ❀ translucent heart token

Shadow stamps are generally solid background stamps that are used to provide an instant backdrop. The most popular shapes are squares or rectangles, which come as single solid blocks, or formations of solid blocks, as featured in this project. Most types of ink can be used with shadow stamps to create a variety of effects.

Here, chalk inks produce a soft, pastel-like look. Colouring pencils are used to highlight the flat images, giving them the illusion of dimension. The heart token and ribbon bow add a novelty touch. This heart design is suitable for a range of occasions, such as a wedding, anniversary or birthday, in appropriate colours.

1 Ink up the set of background blocks with a generous, even layer of orchid ink. Stamp the blocks centrally on the pink folded card, applying firm, even pressure for good contact and an even print. Ink up the stamp and stamp again on a piece of pink card slightly larger than the stamp.

top tip

In shadow stamping, start with the lightest colours, so that you can layer darker stamped images over the top.

2 Select two heart stamps from the set. Using the peony ink, stamp one of the hearts on the top right-hand block and the other on the bottom right-hand block on the pink folded card.

3 Select a third heart stamp from the set. Using the peony ink, stamp the three hearts on alternate blocks on the piece of pink card. Start from the top left-hand block and refer back to the hearts stamped on the folded card to ensure that no two hearts of the same design are next to each other on the finished card.

4 Using the peony ink, stamp the small open block over the left-hand block in the middle row of blocks. Although the open block does not have to be central, stamp it within the orchid block.

5 Using a dark purple colouring pencil, highlight all the hearts on the pink folded card and piece of card. Apply the highlights to the outside edges of the hearts, leaving the centres untouched so that the highlights add a second tone to the hearts.

6 Using the dark purple pencil, add colour to the centre of the open block on the pink folded card. Use the same colour to highlight the corners of the block.

7 Using a white colouring pencil, highlight the corners of the blocks on which the hearts are stamped on the folded card and piece of card. Place the pencil lead on its side to rub white onto the card surface for a softer effect.

8 Using small, sharp scissors, cut out the three heart-stamped blocks from the piece of card. Save the spare blocks for another card.

try this

Ink up and gently press the shadow stamp against a textured surface before stamping. Try corrugated card, mesh or scrunched-up tissue paper.

9 Place small sticky fixers on the backs of the three blocks, one in each corner and one in the centre. Mount the blocks over the corresponding ones on the folded card.

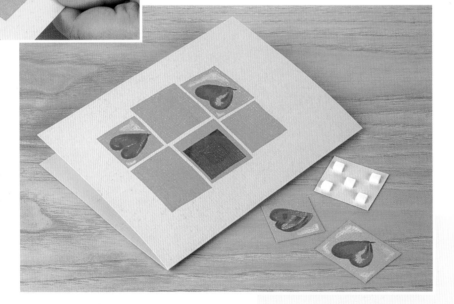

10 Thread a length of ribbon through the hole of the heart token and tie into a double knot to secure. Apply two small dots of PVA glue to the back of the token, avoiding the translucent heart, and stick down over the middle left-hand block.

More ideas
for shadow stamping

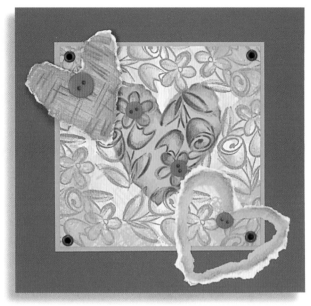

Heart Trio

A heart shadow stamp is the focus of this card. Layers of stamped brushstrokes and flowers are stamped over the top in peach tones and soft red. The flowers stamped over the heart have been highlighted with colouring pencils to make the heart motif stand out. An extra stamped heart has been torn out and then the middle torn out to create a torn heart frame and a smaller torn heart. Brushstrokes have been stamped over the central heart in soft red. These hearts are mounted over the edges of the central panel to give the card a less formal look. Tiny buttons and eyelets provide decorative accents.

Butterflies & Flowers

This long border of blocks is an ideal layout for mini stamps, with the dainty butterflies stamped as though dancing along the blocks. Layers of blue, starting with the palest for the background and darkest on the flowers and butterflies, bring depth to the design. Colouring pencils are used to add highlights to the wings and petals. To carry the theme through, the stamped border is mounted on a light blue panel and onto a folded deep blue card. Brads make excellent flower centres.

Button Flowers

Shadow stamps come not just in blocks but a variety of shapes and they are not even always solid. On this card, a flower shadow stamp is combined with an open flower. The background is made up of pale brushstroke marks that are actually stamped. Colouring pencils are used to build up the layers further and a flower stem stamp adds decorative detail. The stamped lines have been gone over with colouring pencils for a hand-drawn effect and extra depth. Some flowers have been stamped on a spare background piece, cut out and raised on the card with sticky fixers. The buttons contribute an element of fun.

Chalks

You Will Need

- 🌼 cream card
- 🌼 pale green folded card 16.5 x 12cm (6½ x 4¾in)
- 🌼 decorating chalks
- 🌼 VersaMark™ inkpad
- 🌼 large and small pressed wild flower stamps
- 🌼 1/16 in hole punch
- 🌼 yellow sheer ribbon
- 🌼 4 pale green 1/8 in brads

Chalks are perfect for creating a soft, subtle finish and are suitable for use with both solid and open stamps. With solid stamps, the image is stamped with a clear ink such as VersaMark™. The chalks are then dusted onto the surface of the image with cotton wool. With open stamps, chalks can be used either to colour the outline or inside the image.

Chalks are ideally suited to conveying the delicate quality of pressed flowers in this design. The cream background card tones down the chalk colours and the base card is appropriately muted in tone and textured.

1 Before you begin stamping, it is best to prepare the first layer of chalk to be applied to the stamped flowers. Take a small ball of cotton wool and rub it gently on the surface of the yellow chalk block. Avoid pressing too hard on the chalk block as they break easily. Set aside the cotton wool ball.

2 Cut a piece of cream card 13.5 x 9cm (5¼ x 3½in). Using the inkpad and the large stamp, stamp three flowers onto the centre of the cream card. Stamp the middle flower first, keeping the stem as straight as possible. Stamp the other two flowers in a cross formation over the first one.

3 Using the chalked cotton wool ball, very gently dust yellow chalk all over the stamped flowers. This layer highlights the flowers, making it easier to see where to apply the subsequent layers of chalk. If too much pressure is applied, the image may be rubbed off or smudged.

top tip

Look at real flowers or pictures in books and magazines to get some ideas on colour. Some flowers are hard to colour and following an example is sometimes easier, especially if you want them to look realistic.

4 Using the lightest colours first, gradually build up the layers of chalk over the flowers. On the flower heads, keep the tips of the petals light and the centre dark. On the stems, use dark green sparingly as a highlight. When small amounts of colour need to be applied to a specific area, a cotton bud can be used. As a cotton bud is harder, apply as little pressure as possible to avoid removing rather than adding chalk.

5 When all the layers of chalks have been added, use a clean cotton wool ball to dust over the entire image. This will remove most of the chalk residue. There will be a faint halo of colour left around the flowers. Leave this to enhance the background.

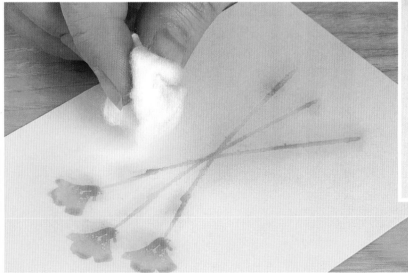

6 Tear away the edges of the card around the image, tearing towards you to reveal the layers of the card. Dust layers of light green chalk all over the torn edges. Add highlights of dark green chalk at random. Remove any residue with a clean cotton wool ball.

7 Cut a rectangle of cream card measuring 16 x 11.5cm (6¼ x 4½in). Using the inkpad and the small stamp, stamp small flowers at random all around the edges of the card. Using the same colours, repeat the chalking process used for the large flowers. Tear away the edges of the card as in Step 6. Dust the torn edges with orange and vermilion chalk.

8 Using the hole punch, make a hole either side of where the stalks cross through the card. If the punch does not reach, use an 'anywhere' hole punch if you have one or otherwise a compass point or large needle. Thread the sheer ribbon through the holes and tie into a bow at the front.

9 Direct a heat gun at the ribbon bow, holding it not less than 5cm (2in) away, and carefully heat. This will crinkle the ribbon. Do not use this technique without experimenting first, as some types of ribbon may not react in the same way. Using spray glue, mount the smaller card panel centrally onto the larger one, then mount centrally onto the pale green folded card. Open out the card. Using the hole punch, make a hole in each corner of the larger card panel through the card front and insert a brad in each hole (see page 37).

SMART STAMPING
Chalks

✔ You can use artists' chalk pastels instead by rubbing the chalk onto paper and picking up the colour from the paper.

✔ There are many different tools for applying chalks, including sponge applicators and Fantastix™ brush or bullet tips (see page 33). Experiment with the various kinds of applicators and chalks to find a combination that works best for you.

✔ As no water is involved in the colouring process, chalks can be successfully used with dye-based inkpads on paper and card. If the paper or card is matt and slightly textured, it will help the chalks to key onto the surface.

✔ Chalks can be applied to a variety of stamping surfaces, including shrink plastic and cork, as well as fabric, provided that it is not going to be washed.

More ideas for chalks

Sail Away

Chalks are particularly good for colouring in landscapes or seascapes, as on this card, since the colours can be easily blended, which is especially useful for creating skies. Although the chalk colours are naturally soft, they also have a freshness, so that here they convey the feeling of a breeze blowing off the sea. The torn edges of the panel and background strip add to the weather-worn look. A charm in the form of a ship's wheel and string tied in a knot make perfect nautical embellishments.

Daisy Bear

Chalks are ideal for this sweet little bear sitting down with her potted daisy, softening the outline of the bear's fur and bringing a delicate quality to the bloom. The panel is turned into a pretend tag with the addition of a single snap to the top. To make an interesting border, the yellow card on which the main panel is layered has been torn in the same way as the panel. The tag is mounted onto a tall white folded card with a printed vellum panel, its daisies co-ordinating nicely with the daisy in the flowerpot.

Christmas Robins

The chalks on this card have been used in two different ways, first to colour the stamped outlines of the robins and the holly, and secondly to add tone and shading to the leaves, berries and the birds' bodies. The softness of the chalks emphasizes the fluffy feathers of the baby robins and also gives the whole image a frosty winter look. A touch of glitter on the holly leaves also contributes to the wintry effect. Adding pale green vellum and transparent sheer ribbon to the layering of the image subdues the strong red and green card used for mounting.

Sponged Backgrounds

You Will Need

- magenta square Mosaic Sheet™
- red patterned paper
- blue folded card 16.5 x 11cm (6½ x 4¼ in)
- blue card
- icicles VersaColor™ multicoloured pigment inkpad
- Sponge Dauber™
- dynamic Vivid™ Rainbow Dye inkpad
- sketched blossoms stamp
- square punch
- tag punch
- ⅛in hole punch
- red cord
- red metal heart

Sponging is ideal for creating soft, muted backgrounds. Often the same inks are used for both the background and the stamped image, for effective co-ordination. Use a tight, rounded sponge to avoid creating lines and gradually build up the layers of ink, starting with the lightest shade.

Here, a sponged background has been stamped with a sketched flower image using a multicoloured inkpad. For an extra twist, the background paper is made up of self-adhesive tiles, which are then separated after stamping.

1 Using the icicles inkpad, load up the Sponge Dauber™ with the two lightest blue shades. Simply press the Sponge Dauber™ gently down onto the surface of the inkpad. Always test out the dauber on scrap paper before using just in case too much ink has been picked up.

2 Cut two pieces from the Mosaic Sheet™ 5 x 3 squares. Sponge both pieces with the two shades of blue ink, leaving gaps in the sponging to add the extra shades later. Re-load the dauber when all the ink on it is used up. This will help achieve the mottled effect.

top tip

If you don't have a Sponge Dauber™ or a suitable sponge available, use small inkpads to apply the ink direct to the paper.

3 Load the dauber with the next two shades of blue on the icicles inkpad. Fill in the gaps on the mosaic papers. Try not to over-sponge at this stage, to avoid lessening the mottled effect.

top tip

If you are making several cards in one go, sponge a whole sheet of ordinary paper or Mosaic Sheet™ at a time.

4 Using the red to light blue section of the rainbow inkpad, ink up the blossom stamp, pressing the stamp down onto the surface of the pads and moving over the same colour bands, but avoiding too much movement from side to side. Stamp the image centrally on one mosaic paper, then re-ink and stamp again on the second paper.

5 Carefully lift the tiles from the backing sheet one at a time, starting from one of the corners.

6 Cut a piece of the patterned paper 15 x 9.5cm (6 x 3¾in). Place the first corner tile of one of the mosaic papers in the top left-hand corner of the background paper, leaving a border above and to the left 6mm (¼in) wide. Cut a strip of card 4mm (⅛in) wide to act as a spacer. Place the spacer next to the first tile, hold down and add the next tile. Repeat the process until all the tiles are laid. Using spray glue, mount the tile panel centrally on the blue folded card.

7 Turn the square punch upside down. Place one of the tiles from the second mosaic paper into the punch. Punch out the chosen area. Keep the leftover mosaic squares for another card.

try this

The Mosaic Sheets™ come with other shaped tiles, such as triangles and diamonds, and in different sizes to create a variety of designs. Sheets of self-adhesive frames are also available.

8 Place the punched square on a small rectangle of blue card. Turn the tag punch upside down, place the card inside the punch and line up so that the square appears in the opening at the base of the tag. Punch out the tag.

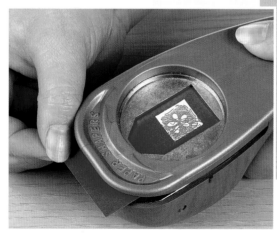

9 Using the hole punch, make a hole in the top of the tag. Cut a length of red cord and thread through the hole as in a luggage tag. Untwist the ends of the cord to make them fray. Using PVA glue, stick the red metal heart onto the square. Using sticky fixers, mount the tag onto the bottom left-hand corner of the card.

More ideas
for sponged backgrounds

Loving Giraffes

A piece of cream card has been sponged with browns to create an earthy background for the giraffes. The giraffes have been stamped onto the sponged background using a tiramisu Brilliance™ inkpad. This pad is made up of beige, brown and black bands, which are perfect for the animal markings. For a natural look, the edges of the sponged card are torn. The panel is mounted on a cream card pre-stamped with an ethnic pattern to complement the theme of the card.

Orchid Beauties

With experience, subtle, multicoloured backgrounds can be achieved with sponging. Soft colours are particularly suitable for flower images, and on this card, soft pink, mint and yellow inks have been sponged across a piece of mosaic paper. Stamped images have then been layered on top of the sponged background – these should always be applied from light to dark in colour or shade – including an undefined script, which creates an interesting effect. The final stamped image is like a collage. Three small square plastic tiles highlight some of the detail on the orchid panel. A length of sheer ribbon adds the finishing touch.

Tulips All In a Row

A piece of mosaic paper has been sponged with yellow, lime and green ink. A second layer of flowers has been stamped across the mosaic paper using a multicoloured inkpad. The row of tulips has been created with one stamp individually inked and stamped three times. With each layer, the colours intensify. To anchor the tulips, a torn strip of yellow vellum is attached to the card with red eyelets. The colours of the cards used to create a layered frame around the image echo the colour scheme of the tile panel.

Bleaching Out

You Will Need

- blue card
- pale yellow vellum
- white folded card 12 x 17cm (4¾ x 6¾in)
- bouquet and dragonfly stamps
- royal blue pigment inkpad
- clear embossing powder
- thick household bleach
- soft-leaded colouring pencils
- tag punch
- ⅛in hole punch
- 1⁄16 in hole punch
- 4 pale blue ⅛in brads
- yellow sheer ribbon
- peel-off stickers: gold butterflies

Bleach is a versatile painting medium. It can be used to produce different shades of one colour in a stamped image for a monochromatic effect. Alternatively, use it to remove colour from the background card or paper, which then allows you to work with colours that might otherwise be lost on the strong background while retaining the full impact of the colour as a backdrop.

The blue card in this project would have overwhelmed the softer pencil colours of the flowers, but the bleach provides a neutral base for colouring without sacrificing the vibrancy of the background. Dainty butterflies and a ribbon bow complete the delightfully summery picture.

1 Stamp and emboss one bouquet and one dragonfly on blue card using the blue inkpad and clear embossing powder – make sure that the piece of card for the bouquet is large enough for the image to be torn out. Be careful to remove any unwanted specks of embossing powder before heating with the heat gun.

top tip

The outline of a stamped image does not always have to be black. For a less stark contrast, choose a colour that works with the look of the card. Dark blue or brown outlines give a softer effect.

2 Cover your work surface to protect it, then carefully pour just a couple of drops of full-strength bleach into an old thick, rigid plastic lid or shallow ceramic container. Using a paintbrush, paint the bleach over the bouquet. Be careful not to go over the outline onto the background or the lines within the image. The bleach will remove the blue dye from the card, making it almost white.

3 Colour in the bouquet using colouring pencils. Try using two shades of each colour to give the image depth. Using a white pencil, add highlights to the leaves, fruit and flowers.

4 Tear away the edges of the card around the bouquet, tearing towards you to reveal the layers of the card. To make sure all the torn edges are identical, work in a clockwise rotation.

6 Using spray glue, mount the bouquet panel on a slightly larger piece of pale yellow vellum. Tear the edges of the vellum to leave a small border all the way round the panel. The border can be uneven, since this will add to the finished effect.

5 Using a white pencil, highlight the background of the bouquet. Place the pencil lead on its side and gently rub colour over the card. Try to apply varied pressure on the lead to achieve a mottled background. Leave the area around the outline of the bouquet unshaded.

7 Bleach out the colour on the wings of the dragonfly. Using a white pencil, highlight the area around the outline of the dragonfly. Turn the tag punch upside down and slip the dragonfly into the punch. Select the area for the tag and punch out. Punch an additional tag from the pale yellow vellum. Using the ⅛in hole punch, make a hole in the top of each tag.

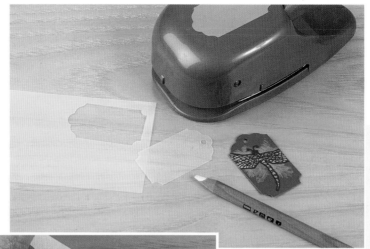

8 Mount the completed panel on the front of the white folded card. Open out the card. Using the 1/16in hole punch, make a hole in each corner of the blue panel through the card and insert a brad in each hole (see page 37). Using the ⅛in hole punch, make two further holes on either side of the flower stems. Thread a length of ribbon from the back of the card front through the holes in the panel to the front. Thread on the dragonfly tag, then the vellum tag and tie the ribbon in a bow.

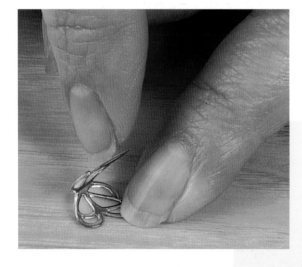

9 Place two butterfly peel-off stickers on pale yellow vellum. Using small, sharp scissors, cut out the butterflies. Carefully fold them in half, with right sides together.

top tip

The effects of the bleaching out technique will vary according to the card and paper quality, so try it out on different types to find one that gives you the best results.

try this

Use this technique for natural motifs and designs, to replicate the subtle gradations of colour that occur in nature, such as in leaves and flowers.

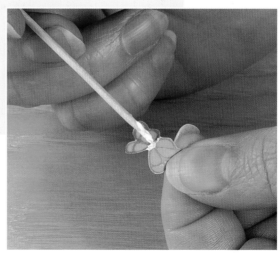

10 Holding a butterfly upside down, apply PVA glue to the fold. Use a cocktail stick to apply the glue accurately and sparingly. Stick the butterfly on the card. Repeat the process with the second butterfly and stick in place.

More ideas for bleaching out

Wire Leaves

Careful and varied application of bleach has created the various tones on this card. Two images were stamped on burgundy card and bleached out, one forming the base panel and the other providing leaves for cutting out. The latter have been raised and attached with sticky fixers. Cream card frames the central panel and the same burgundy card used for the leaves provides a further layer, to match the colouring of the central design. Small leaf-shaped burgundy buttons add an extra decorative element.

Sunflower Teddy

This cute teddy was stamped on light brown card using a brown inkpad before bleach was applied over his body to lighten the fur and over the sunflower head to lighten the card colour. Colouring pencils have been used to add tone and shading to the sunflower head, stalk and leaves. A tall folded card and punched out tag have been covered with paper that mimics corrugated card. The yellow torn border picks up the colour of the sunflower. Wooden ladybirds add a fun dimension and the raffia co-ordinates with the scheme.

Purple Blossoms

The blossoms were stamped with black ink on purple card. Bleach was then applied to the flower heads, buds and leaves to remove the purple die. The background was left untouched, with only white pencil applied at the colouring-in stage. A torn strip of pale pink vellum was folded over part of the stamped panel before it was stuck to a pale pink folded card. Two metal eyelets secure the vellum to the card. Oriental-style embellishments would work well with this design.

Embossing Pens

You Will Need

- honey yellow card
- black card
- mango folded card 12cm (4¾in) square
- black, marigold and orange pigment inkpads
- leaf and pumpkin stamps
- black and clear embossing powders
- 2 shades of green, orange and brown dual embossing pens
- Sponge Daubers™
- ¹⁄₁₆ in hole punch
- wire cutters
- 22-gauge copper wire
- kebab stick
- peel-off sticker: black eyelet
- orange sheer ribbon

Embossing pens contain slow-drying ink that allows you time to colour in an image and emboss it. Any colour embossing powder can be used, although the clear ones will obviously let the colours show through. Available in four different tips – bullet, brush and small and large chisel – these pens can also be used for freehand lettering and drawing. The pen colours are so bold that they are best combined with strong, graphic images.

The range of autumnal shades in this card, including the copper wire and orange ribbon, work particularly well with the strong black embossed outlines of the motifs. A clear embossing powder is used to cover the leaves and sections of the pumpkin, which have been coloured with the pens.

1 Cut a piece of honey yellow card 10cm (4in) square and place on some scrap paper. Using the black inkpad, stamp leaves all over the card, creating a random pattern. Stamp the leaves over the edges of the card. Sprinkle black embossing powder all over the card, shake off the excess and heat with a heat gun to emboss. Brush any stray black specks away with a fine paintbrush before heating.

2 Using the embossing pens, colour in the leaves – one leaf of the pair in the two shades of green and the other in orange and brown. Apply the lightest colour first to avoid contaminating the pen nibs and use the wetness of the pens to blend the colours where they meet.

top tip

Sponge Daubers™ are best for applying the ink, since their dome shape prevents any streaks or lines being left. They can be washed to remove the ink when you need to use another colour.

3 Colour four to five leaves at a time and cover with the clear embossing powder. Although the pens contain slow-drying ink, it is best and easier to colour and emboss sections of the design at a time.

4 Heat the embossing powder until it has melted. Allow to cool before continuing to colour the leaves. Keep repeating the process until the whole panel is complete.

6 Cut a piece of honey yellow card 6.5 x 6cm (2½ x 2⅜in). Cut off two adjacent corners to form a tag shape. Using the hole punch, make a hole in the top of the tag. Using the black inkpad and black embossing powder, stamp and emboss the pumpkin on the tag.

5 Starting with the lightest orange inkpad and using a Sponge Dauber™, sponge the ink over the panel in the gaps between the leaves. Add the darker orange in the same way, but this time apply less of it to allow the previous layer to show through. Using spray glue, mount the panel on a slightly larger piece of black card, then mount on the mango folded card at an angle.

7 Using the embossing pens, colour in the pumpkin, leaving some areas of the pumpkin uncovered for a contemporary effect. Use the orange to cover most areas of the pumpkin and touches of brown to add shading on the outer edges.

8 Using the hole punch, make a hole either side of the pumpkin stalk.

try this

Bold, contemporary effects can be achieved by using embossing pens with transparent glitter and holographic embossing powders.

9 Using wire cutters, cut a short length of copper wire and bend it into a hairpin shape. Thread the ends of the wire through the holes in the tag from the back to the front.

10 Curl one end of the wire at a time around a kebab stick to create a coil. Keep the coiling loose, and once the stick is removed, pull some of the coils together and squeeze some apart. Fold and push the coils over each other and up against the surface of the tag. Sponge marigold and orange ink over the edges of the tag. Place a peel-off eyelet over the tag hole. Tie a length of ribbon to the tag and mount centrally on the card with sticky fixers

More ideas
for embossing pens

Pink Elephant

This little elephant stamp is ideal for a young child's birthday card. For this card it has been coloured pink to suit a little girl, but it could easily be in blue for a boy. The colour scheme has been kept simple, limited mainly to pinks and purples. Both the elephant and the number five have been coloured using a pink embossing pen and covered with clear embossing powder. The elephant on the stamp is actually holding a rattle, but if inappropriate, it can be covered up with another element, such as the flower head button in this case. A stencil made from a punched flower has been used to create the background pattern behind the elephant.

Ladybirds & Daisies

To make the ladybirds stand out, a red embossing pen was used to colour them in before they were embossed with clear powder. A large tag punch was then turned upside down in order to centre the ladybirds within the shape. As the layer of embossing powder acts as a protective barrier, it is possible to sponge ink close to the ladybirds. The various shades of green ink used on the tags make the ladybirds stand out even more because of the contrast in colour values. Daisy head stickers have been used to decorate the dark green background panel on which the tags are mounted.

How Does Your Garden Grow?

This design of three bold, graphic flowers is perfectly suited to the bright colours of embossing pens. The image was stamped and embossed on white card using a black inkpad and black embossing powder. Once the flowers had been coloured in and embossed, the background was sponged using green, yellow and orange inks applied with Sponge Daubers™. A spare flower was stamped and embossed to create the tag. Small punched flowers make an additional border and a ladybird button adds a fun embellishment.

Multi Embossing

You Will Need

- turquoise and purple pearlescent card
- turquoise pearlescent folded card 15 x 12cm (6 x 4¾in)
- amethyst, ruby and sapphire PearlLustre™ embossing powders
- Clear Emboss™ or VersaMark™ inkpad
- peacock feather and crackle-glaze background stamps
- tiny rectangular punch
- beads
- silver thread
- blue acrylic gem

Embossing with a single powder is straightforward, but when you start to use more than one colour, the outcome is rather more unpredictable – and exciting! The application of the powder needs to be more precise and controlled for successful results. The PearlLustre™ range of embossing powders, used here, offers great colours that mostly work well together. A variety of effects can be achieved by using different-coloured card and inkpads.

The multi-embossing treatment particularly lends itself to this design, as the colours on a feather vary and they are not too specifically distributed, but many other images are suitable, such as leaves, flowers and hearts. The pearlescent card co-ordinates with the powders and metallic beads provide the perfect embellishment.

1 Choose a maximum of three differently coloured pearlescent powders that will work well together and are in keeping with the peacock feather subject matter, such as those specified above. Using a Clear Emboss™ or VersaMark™ inkpad, stamp the peacock feather on a piece of turquoise pearlescent card 11 x 4.5cm (4¼ x 1¾in). The image will be virtually invisible, so you will need to handle the card with care.

2 Using a small scoop, sprinkle small quantities of the first embossing powder colour at random over the feather. Be sure to leave gaps for the other colours. The first layer of powder will make it easier to see the image. You can apply the three colours in any order, but bear in mind that the last colour usually has the least coverage.

top tip

Label any new combinations of embossing powder you end up with, as you may not remember or recognize the contents later.

3 Shake off the excess powder by the shortest route to keep the coverage to a minimum. The powder can be returned to its original container. Remove any unwanted specks with a fine paintbrush.

4 Sprinkle the second colour over the feather and remove the excess as in Step 3. However, the excess from this layer may be contaminated, so put it in a new, separate container, but keep it and you will have a new embossing powder! Repeat the whole process with the third colour. Handle the card with care until you have heat embossed the design.

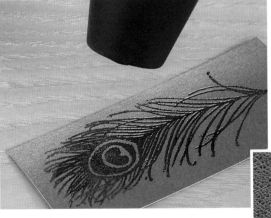

5 Using a heat gun, heat the surface of the powder until it has melted. Using spray glue, mount the design on a slightly larger piece of purple pearlescent card.

6 Cut a piece of turquoise pealescent card 13.5 x 10.5cm (5¼ x 4¼ in). Stamp the crackle-glaze background onto the card, applying a good amount of pressure, and emboss as before using the same ink and powders.

7 Mount the background on a slightly larger piece of purple pearlescent card. Measure and mark 2.5cm (1in) from the right-hand edge on the top and bottom edges of the background. Using the rectangular punch, punch a notch at each mark in the purple border.

top tip

Multi embossing works well with both open and solid stamps, but use fine-grained embossing powders for more intricate designs to avoid losing the detail.

8 Thread several beads onto a length of silver thread. Use a needle if the beads have very small holes.

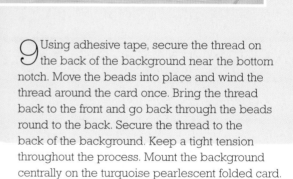

9 Using adhesive tape, secure the thread on the back of the background near the bottom notch. Move the beads into place and wind the thread around the card once. Bring the thread back to the front and go back through the beads round to the back. Secure the thread to the back of the background. Keep a tight tension throughout the process. Mount the background centrally on the turquoise pearlescent folded card.

10 Using a cocktail stick, dab a small quantity of PVA glue onto the centre of the 'eye' of the peacock feather. Carefully position the gem over the glue. When the glue has dried, use sticky fixers to mount the feather panel onto the left-hand side of the background.

More ideas
for multi embossing

African Daisy

This daisy stamp, which is virtually a solid image, is perfect for multi embossing, and lends itself to lots of different colour schemes. The brown, orange and gold powders used to emboss the daisy on this card have inspired an African theme, emphasized by the pattern stamped on the background panel and the wooden bead. Contrast is created by having both torn and straight edges on the various panels. Thin wire has been used to attach the bead to the gold panel, the curled ends providing an extra decorative element. By limiting the colour range, a striking, stylish design has been produced.

Autumn Leaves

Four embossing powders were used to create these autumn-coloured leaves, stamped on a green pearlescent panel. Once embossed, the background between the leaves has been lightly sponged. Another single leaf was stamped and embossed on similar card, and an area of the leaf punched out. Both the large panel and the punched square are mounted on copper card in keeping with the autumn hues. Tiny Diamond Dots™ highlight the central leaf and copper snaps make a decorative border.

Oriental Kimono

Multi embossing is great for creating colour variations in patterns, such as those on the kimono and the background panel. The kimono has been stamped and embossed on lilac pearlescent card using three different powders, then cut out and mounted on a blue pearlescent panel, stamped with a large background stamp. Sticky fixers raise the kimono and make it the focus of the design, while the gold card used for mounting and the kimono sash enriches the colours. Domed gems make a perfect embellishment, tying in with the oriental theme.

Masking

In this easy but impressive technique, a mask is used to cover and protect a stamped image from ink when further images are being stamped over it. In this way, groups of a single, overlapping image can be stamped to create a more interesting design, such as a bunch of balloons or a bouquet of flowers – a great way to get extra creative mileage out of your stamps. Masking can also be used to create backgrounds and to stamp into a window or frame (see page 27).

The masking technique is exploited to the full in these prancing zebras, stamped using a multicoloured inkpad, to create a strong three-dimensional design. The raffia, wire and beads, in keeping with the African safari theme, enhance the spatial effect.

You Will Need

- white parchment card
- black card
- sandstone folded card 9 x 20cm (3½ x 8in)
- primrose Ancient Page™ inkpad
- zebra and leaf stamps
- stick-on notepad
- tiramisu and coffee bean Brilliance™ inkpads
- clingfilm
- raffia
- ¹⁄₁₆ in hole punch
- 26-gauge copper wire
- 1 large and 2 small beads

1 Using the primrose inkpad, stamp the zebra on the stick-on notepad – it is important to use permanent ink that will not bleed if it becomes wet. Make sure part of the image is stamped over the sticky band at the top of the pad – in this case the hooves – which will hold the mask in place. Use small, sharp scissors to cut out the zebra mask.

top tip

When cutting out a mask, don't try to cut out details of the image that are very fine and flimsy, such as the zebra's tail in this case, since they will only break off when using the mask.

3 When the ink on the first zebra is dry, cover it with the mask, checking that it is stuck down at the hooves. Stamp the second zebra so that its back legs are bucking up in the middle of the card. Its back legs should overlap the front legs of the first zebra.

2 Cut a piece of white parchment card 8 x 19cm (3¼ x 7½in). Using the tiramisu inkpad, ink up the zebra so that the lightest colour is on the back legs. The order of colouring can be reversed, but keep it the same for all three zebras or the inkpad will get messed up. Stamp the first zebra so that it is rearing up on its back legs at the left-hand end of the white card.

5 Place the card on scrap paper. Loosely roll together a piece of clingfilm to make a small finger pad. Use this to dab ink around the edges of the panel. Apply the lightest colour from the tiramisu inkpad first, building up to the darkest. The pad will create a dusty, grassy effect.

4 Check that the ink is dry on the second zebra and the mask before continuing to avoid smudges and fingerprints. Cover the second zebra with the mask and stamp the third zebra in the gap remaining on the card so that it is rearing up on its back legs. The tail of the third zebra should overlap the front legs of the second zebra. Remove the mask and store away for future use.

6 Using the coffee inkpad, stamp the leaves at random over the edges of the card. Rotate the stamp to vary the pattern. Try to fit the leaves into the gaps between the zebras' legs and heads.

7 Using a cocktail stick, apply a short line of PVA glue towards the left-hand end of the bottom edge of the card. Cut several pieces of raffia varying in length. Position each piece over the glue and press down for a good bond. Do not worry if any glue is visible, as it will dry clear. Stick the tips of the raffia down to make an interesting arrangement. Repeat the process at two further spaced intervals across the bottom of the card to make two more bushes.

8 Using small, sharp scissors, trim off any excess raffia at the base of the card. Using spray glue, mount the card centrally onto a slightly larger piece of black card, then centrally onto the sandstone folded card.

top tip

Strong-bonding PVA glue, such as Hi-Tack Glue™, is relatively slow drying, but its flexibility prevents bulkier items such as beads, wire and raffia from falling off the card when it is handled.

9 Open the card out. Using the hole punch, make four vertically placed holes through the card front on the left-hand side, spacing the holes to match the size of the beads. The space between the second hole and third one is the longest. Thread a length of wire through the first hole from the front, bring it back to the front through the second hole, thread on a bead and loop the wire back through the first hole. Pull on the ends to secure the bead in place. Repeat for the next two beads. Curl the ends around a cocktail stick to complete.

SMART STAMPING
Masking

✔ Stamp the image for the mask in a contrasting colour to the final stamped design, so that you can easily pick out the mask from the stamped design.

✔ When cutting out a mask, remember to cut into the outline or solid image to prevent a halo effect where a gap occurs in between the overlapping images due to stamping over two levels.

✔ Always use lightweight paper for the mask or use special masking film.

✔ Trim the mask down further if you cannot see the outer edges of the stamped image under the mask.

More ideas for masking

Torn Paper

This card is a great example of how various forms of masking can be used to create the illusion of layers. The image for which several masks were created is the aperture with torn flaps. By stamping contrasting images inside and over the top of the aperture, depth is immediately created. Sponging in the background gives further dimension and makes the torn flaps look as if they really are sticking up. To add interest, part of a lady's face has been stamped through one aperture. The subtle colour scheme makes the paper appear aged and worn.

Butterfly Blocks

Backgrounds can be difficult to colour in or paint around stamped images. Using masking and sponging is a simple way of overcoming this problem. For this card, two masks have been used to create the blocks. Blue inks have been sponged over the butterfly mask and the frame mask. The process has been repeated three times to create three small butterfly pictures. The background around each butterfly has a soft, air-brushed look. The blue theme is carried through to the folded card, which has been stamped with script butterflies.

Yellow Roses

Without the masking it would have been impossible to overlap these roses and leaves unless they were cut out and stuck on the card. Where a mask is simple enough to cut out, as in this case, you can stamp new arrangements to create completely fresh images. The roses have been stamped on cream card using black ink and coloured in using pencils in shades of yellow, orange and green. The tiny dots on the image help to indicate where to apply the shading and darker tones. Green card is used to layer up the roses and pick up the colours in the leaves. Pale yellow vellum has been added to soften the overall effect.

Cut Away

This useful cutting technique instantly turns an ordinary design into a novelty one, either for special-occasion cards or eye-catching place cards. Choose stamps with simple outlines that are easy to cut around.

Here, because the outline of the stamped image – the teddies' fur – is difficult to cut around, a simplified cutting line is drawn a short distance away from the image. This versatile design could be used as a birth announcement or to celebrate a birth – perhaps even for twins! The colour can be changed to traditional pink for a girl. And such a special card deserves a decorated envelope to match.

1 Cut a piece of white card 10.5 x 14.8cm or A6 format (5½ x 4¼ in). Using the blue inkpad, stamp the teddies centrally on the card and a paw print in each bottom corner.

top tip

When making construction marks on a card (see Steps 2–4), use a pencil with a sharp, hard lead such as a 2H. Pencils with soft leads tend to smudge and the marks are darker. Use a good-quality eraser that does not smudge.

3 Draw a line between the two points with the ruler and pencil. Draw the line as softly as possible and avoid drawing on the teddies.

2 Mark the halfway point on one short side of the card. Use a ruler and hard pencil to make a small mark. Repeat on the other short side.

5 Place the card on a cutting mat. Again using the line going across the middle as the starting and finishing point, cut along the pencil line around the teddies with a craft knife. Keep the cutting action as smooth as possible. Erase all the pencil lines and marks.

4 Using the line going across the card as the starting and finishing point, draw a soft pencil line around the top half of the teddies, 3–4mm (1/8in) away from them and loosely following the outline of the heads – if the line is too wiggly, it will be difficult to cut.

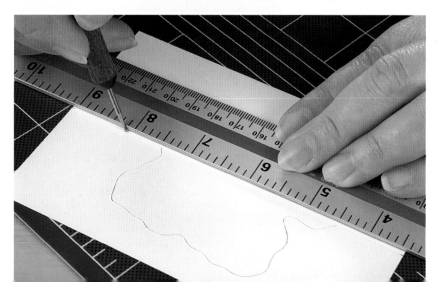

6 Turn the card over and mark the halfway points as in Step 2. Use the fine ball on the dry embossing tool to score a line between the points on either side of the teddies. Use the cut line to see where to start and finish.

top tip

Using the ink from the pad will make for a perfect match with your stamping. When picking up colour directly from the pad, use the edge of the pad, not the centre, and never use a paintbrush dripping with water to avoid the ink becoming over-diluted for subsequent stamping.

7 Using a wet paintbrush, pick up some ink from the blue inkpad. Shade the teddies with soft layers of the ink. Keep the shading on the outer edges of the arms, legs and heads. This will give the teddies a more three-dimensional look.

8 Make sure that the cut line around the teddies has no sections left uncut before carefully folding back the upper half of the card. Fold the card into the crease scored along the back. Use a gel pen to draw a stitched line across the card on either side of the teddies just beneath the fold. Decorate an envelope to match with stamped paw prints and a stitched border.

9 Tie a bow out of a length of ribbon. Stick a tiny blue button onto the knot in the bow, using a strong, flexible PVA glue. Dab the glue onto the bow with a cocktail stick for precision. Using the same glue and cocktail stick, attach the bow in between the two teddies and a button at each outer end of the stitched line on the card.

SMART STAMPING

Cut Away

✔ Always change the blade of a craft knife regularly so that you avoid using a blunt blade that might tear the card.

✔ Try to judge how much pressure is needed to cut the card. If you use too much, you might be cutting too deeply into the mat, causing damage and creating more work than is necessary.

✔ When not in use, if your craft knife doesn't have a retractable blade, stick the blade into a cork to make it safe and to protect it.

More ideas for cut away

Flowers with Love

A single piece of white card was used to create this card, as in the main project, but a portrait format was selected instead to co-ordinate with the shape of the bouquet, which was stamped with a multicoloured dye-based inkpad, along with the butterfly. Inks from the inkpad and colouring pencils were used to colour the image. As well as filling in the open spaces, the pencils were used to emphasize the outline. A vellum strip covers part of the bouquet to soften the effect. A metal heart tag with crinkled ribbon completes the design.

Halloween Ghost

The ghost was stamped on the inside of a white folded card on the back of the front panel, and the right-hand side of the image cut away, up to the fold line down the centre of the image. The ghost was coloured in using grey and black pencils before the right-hand side of the panel was folded under the left, concertina-style. The bats on the inside were stamped directly onto the back panel, but those on the front were stamped on separate card, cut out and raised with sticky fixers. The pumpkin was stamped separately, cut out and added as the ghost's yo-yo, the string drawn in black pen. Sponged grey clouds surround the ghost and bats. Black and orange ribbon decorate the back panel and glitter highlights detail on the ghost, bats and pumpkin.

Bunny Pots

This stamp is very versatile, as the whole image can be used or the little rabbits separately. For this Easter design, the image was stamped across the middle of a piece of cream card and cut away as in the main project. Colouring pencils were used to bring the image to life. The egg shapes were punched out. A piece of green background paper borders the bottom of the card, where additional bunnies and eggs create a fun composition.

3-D Découpage

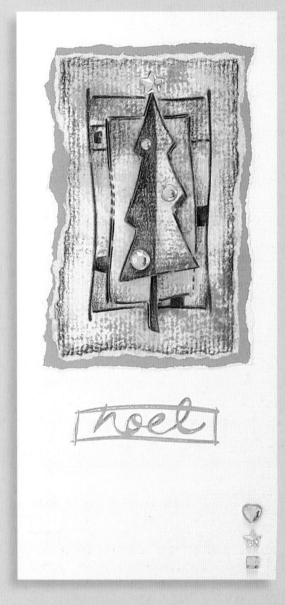

You Will Need

- ❀ white card
- ❀ thin gold card
- ❀ white folded card 18 x 8.5cm (7 x 3¼ in)
- ❀ lime green and olive pastel ColorBox Fluid Chalk™ inkpads
- ❀ framed tree stamp
- ❀ 2 shades of green soft-leaded colouring pencils
- ❀ peel-off sticker: noel
- ❀ pale green self-adhesive acrylic gems

top tip

This 'direct-to-paper' technique can create many different effects, varying according to the surface of the paper, the amount of pressure applied and the type of inkpad used.

As with traditional découpage, 3-D découpage involves cutting out and applying images, but focuses on layering elements of an image to create a three-dimensional design. It works particularly well where images overlap, to enhance the natural spatial effect.

The tree stamp used here is easy to break down into two layers, selecting different elements for each layer. The self-adhesive gems add a further dimension as well as festive sparkle.

1 Dab the lime green inkpad directly all over a large piece of white card. The result will depend on the amount of pressure applied. Do not aim to cover the whole sheet with ink, but allow areas of the white card to show through.

2 Repeat the process in Step 1 using the olive pastel inkpad. As this is a much stronger colour, less ink needs to be applied to the card. Allow quite large gaps in between applications so that the previous layer of inking can show through the breaks.

3 Using the olive pastel inkpad, stamp the tree three times on the background. The images will be quite faint, but this is the required effect – if the outline is too dark, it will be hard to draw over the lines with colouring pencils at the next stage.

4 Study the three images and decide which ones will be the base, first layer and second layer. Make yourself some sort of reminder. On the base, the frame is coloured in using two shades of green – the lighter shade for the areas within the frame and the darker shade for the lines. The aim is to highlight the image, not to colour it all over.

5 Colour the next two layers using the two green pencils. On what will be the second layer, concentrate on colouring the inside line of the frame, the areas around the tree and the edges of the tree. On the first layer, colour only the tree, minus the trunk. Tear out the base image, tearing towards you, and cut away the excess card around the other two images.

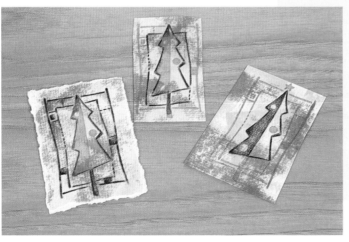

6 Using spray glue, mount the base image on a slightly larger piece of thin gold card. Tear away the edges of the gold card to leave a small border all around the base, tearing towards you to produce a white edge on the gold card. The gold border can be irregular, which will add to the effect.

7 From what will be the second layer, cut out the image along the inside line of the frame. From the first layer, cut around the tree, minus the trunk. Use small, sharp scissors and cut slightly into the frame and tree outline, to make it easier to layer the elements.

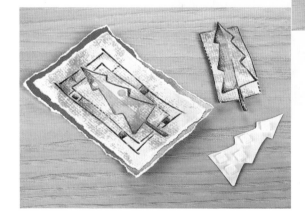

8 Mount the base on the white folded card towards the top. Using sticky fixers, layer the elements on the base, starting with the second layer. It is better to use several small sticky fixers dotted around rather than a few large ones. If all the fixers are only around the edges of the layers, the middle could bow, so make sure the fixers are evenly distributed.

9 Place the noel peel-off sticker on the card below the tree. Using a craft knife, add the gems to the tree and to the bottom right-hand corner of the card.

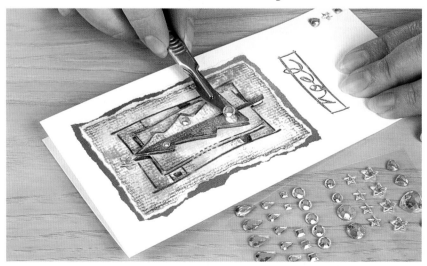

SMART STAMPING

3-D Découpage

✔ Use small, sharp scissors. Nail scissors, straight and curved, are ideal.

✔ Use sticky fixers of varying thicknesses to achieve different depths.

✔ Silicone glue is a viable alternative to sticky fixers, but is heavier and harder to use.

✔ To work out the layering, stamp the image several times on scrap paper and cut out the sections. You can see quickly if it will work or not.

More ideas for 3-D découpage

Daisy Duo

To create the 3-D effect, the flower heads and the background within the frame around the flowers have been raised to make two different layers. The whole image was firstly stamped three times on card stippled with purple and apricot chalk inks. The first image was then cut out leaving a border and used as the base for layering, the second cut out around the frame and only the flower heads used from the third. All the pieces were layered and raised using sticky fixers. The orange and lilac of the folded and background card complement the inks used to stamp the daisies.

Patchwork Hearts

The patchwork hearts image was stamped three times on card previously prepared using the direct-to-paper technique featured in the main project with pink and peony chalk inks. The image breaks down easily into panels and hearts that can be cut out and raised. Extra small hearts were then punched out and added to the design. Pink background paper was stamped with a complementary flower motif. A vellum strip has been wrapped around the front panel of the card and secured with white peel-off sticker eyelets, for further interest.

Polka Dot Vase

Clear stamps were used to stamp the different elements for this flower and vase arrangement. The vase and stalk were originally stamped and embossed using white ink and powder on the background panel. Both were stamped again on other papers, cut out and raised on sticky fixers above those on the panel. The two flower heads were then stamped and embossed on yellow paper, cut out and raised above the vase and stalk. Little punched flowers complete the bouquet. Background papers from the same collection have been used for layering behind the main panel, and a delicate stitched pattern drawn with a fine black pen onto the panel.

Vellum

Vellum is a translucent paper readily available in a variety of thicknesses, colours and patterns. Thinner varieties work well as overlays to soften an image below. However, thicker vellum changes colour when pressure is applied to give a frosted finish. This technique, known as dry embossing, is used in this project.

The pretty dress motif featured on this card is just right for a girl's birthday. The vellum dress has been dry embossed to give a frosted appearance, and seed beads and flower eyelets add the finishing touches.

1 Stamp three dresses on the vellum using the orange inkpad. Leave the ink to dry completely – you can use a heat gun to speed up the process.

top tip

The surface of vellum is non-absorbent, so the ink used must be a fast-drying variety to avoid smudges.

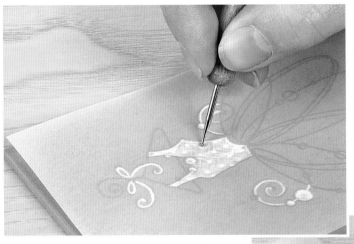

2 Trim a rectangle around one of the dresses – this will be the base dress. Turn the image over and place on the foam mat. Use the dry embossing tool to draw over only the bodice and wire curls. Work over the areas with the tool several times to achieve a raised surface and frosted finish. Use an even pressure to avoid puncturing through the vellum. Draw small dots all over the bodice for decoration.

3 Repeat the process on the second dress image, but this time dry emboss just the skirt. Use lines to emphasize the shape of the skirt. On the third dress image, dry emboss just the two outer sections of the skirt.

4 Using small, sharp scissors, cut out both the complete embossed skirt and the partially embossed skirt. Be aware that vellum is quite brittle, so the skirt will curl up as it is cut out, but this adds to the three-dimensional effect.

5 Starting with the larger piece, stick the skirt layers onto the base dress using dots of PVA glue along the edges of the back of each skirt. Do not apply glue further in than the edges, as this will cause the skirt panels to flatten.

6 Place the Sponge Dauber™ on your index finger and dab on the inkpad to pick up the ink. Sponge the edges of the vellum with orange ink using the Sponge Dauber™. Do not overload the dauber and try to build up the layers evenly.

top tip

To create an instant background for the image, print the stamp onto a subtly patterned pre-printed vellum.

try this

For alternative ways of attaching vellum to card, try using eyelets and brads or ribbon. Vellum can carry a strong crease, so it will wrap firmly around the card.

7 Spray glue over the back of the completed dress panel and mount on a slightly larger piece of white card. Apply the glue to the outside edges only and avoid pushing down on the dress itself. Use the hole punch to make the holes in each corner of the vellum and place a flower eyelet over each.

8 Using spray glue, mount the panel centrally on the orange pearlescent folded card. Stick orange seed beads over the dots on the dress using PVA glue and a cocktail stick.

SMART STAMPING

Vellum

✔ Vellum is ideal for layering over stamped images to create a multi-dimensional, soft effect.

✔ Apply less pressure than usual when pressing down onto vellum, as a stamp can easily skid over the face of the smooth surface.

✔ Always choose a thick, strong variety of vellum if you are dry embossing, to reduce the risk of puncturing the surface and spoiling the paper.

More ideas for vellum

Pink Angel

For this spiritual design, an angel was stamped on pastel pink card and coloured using shades of the same ink. The ink was lifted from the inkpad with a wet brush and layered up. A second angel was stamped on pink vellum and layered directly on top of the first one to soften the colours. The vellum was secured in place with gold brads, then dots of Liquid Pearl™ added to highlight the angel. A trailing pink bow completes the look.

Wedding Bells

Vellum is a perfect material for wedding cards – it complements perfectly the rich silks and organza fabrics associated with weddings. The bells, ribbon and flowers in this design were dry embossed and the edges of the vellum torn. Background dots were dry embossed to give a lacy appearance. The edges were sponged and gems added for decoration. A thinner piece of vellum was stamped, folded and wrapped around the card, and secured to the back with a peel-off sticker to match those in the corners on the front.

Hello Baby

Printed vellums are increasingly popular. A piece of vellum printed with white flowers is used as a background layer – the white pattern shows up clearly against the blue card. The vellum was cut slightly smaller than the card and secured in place with metal brads. The pram was dry embossed and the image punched out with a scalloped square punch before being mounted on white card. Dots of white Liquid Pearl™ were applied to the pram and corners of the scalloped square. A pretty ribbon adds the finishing touch.

Pearlescent Effects

A soft, shimmering effect can be produced with pearlescent paint powders, dusted over an image stamped with a sticky clear ink, to which they will adhere. Although any stamp can be used, solid stamps with bold motifs are the most effective for this technique. For open stamps, the powders are best mixed with water to create a paint medium.

These paint powders are perfect for bringing a brush-like quality to this oriental lily, stamped on black card for maximum impact. The gold frame, Chinese characters and bamboo border work both with the nature of the theme and the design approach.

You Will Need

- ❀ black card
- ❀ gold card
- ❀ raspberry pearlescent folded card 14.5cm (5¾in) square
- ❀ lily stamp
- ❀ VersaMark™ or Perfect Medium™ inkpad
- ❀ Perfect Pearls™: blush, rust, kiwi, sunflower sparkle, turquoise
- ❀ textured sponge stippler
- ❀ peel-off stickers: brads, Chinese characters and gold bamboo border
- ❀ VersaMark™ pen

1 Cut a piece of black card 13.5.x 8cm (5¼ x 3¼in). Using the clear inkpad, turn the stamp over and ink up carefully. Check that there is ink all over the rubber – with clear ink, it is easy to miss areas.

top tip

Before stamping, get the ink powders and brushes ready – although the ink is not fast drying, it is best to add the powders while the image is still fresh.

2 Stamp the lily centrally onto the piece of black card.

3 Working over scrap paper, apply one powder at a time using a small paintbrush – blush and rust for the flower, kiwi for the leaves and sunflower sparkle for highlights. Use a gentle dabbing motion to apply the powders rather than a sweeping one to avoid the stamped image being smudged. Cover the entire image generously.

4 Once the image is entirely covered, start dusting. Using a large paintbrush, brush away one colour at a time, working from the inside to the outside. Occasionally shake off the excess dust from the brush. The image will become sharper as more layers of powder are removed.

5 Using a textured sponge stippler, pick up some ink from the clear inkpad and apply to the background areas around the flower. Be careful not to touch the surface of the flower with the sponge, as this could remove some of the powder.

6 Using the same technique as in Steps 3 and 4, apply the turquoise powder to the areas that have been sponged, then dust off. Avoid dusting the powder over the flower as the excess is removed, since this could contaminate the layers previously applied to the flower.

try this

Add Perfect Pearls™ to clear embossing powder to create a pearlescent colour or knead into air-drying clay to give it a pearlescent sheen.

7 Mount the panel on a slightly larger piece of gold card. Add a brad peel-off sticker to each corner of the panel and the Chinese characters to the bottom right-hand corner. Use a craft knife to lift the embellishments from their sheets and to position them with accuracy.

top tip

Similar products to Perfect Pearls™ are available on the market. Read the instructions carefully before using these products to check if they are compatible with this technique.

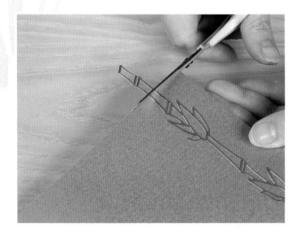

8 Lift a bamboo border from its sheet and position down the right-hand side of the raspberry pearlescent folded card. Trim off the excess with scissors.

9 Using the VersaMark™ pen, colour the open areas of the bamboo. Since it is difficult to see what has been coloured, apply the ink systematically. Apply the sunflower sparkle powder to the bamboo and dust off as in Steps 3 and 4. Using spray glue, mount the flower panel to the left-hand side of the folded card.

More ideas
for pearlescent effects

Golden Pear

Perfect Pearls™ have been used to create both the pear and dragonfly background on this card. The pear was stamped on black card with a Perfect Medium™ inkpad and the pearlescent powders applied. For added interest, small holographic peel-off stickers in the shape of diamonds and dots have been added. The same approach has been used on the pink background card, but the effect is different due to the reaction of the Perfect Pearls™ with the light colour. Pearlescent card is an ideal complement to the colour treatment. The completed panel has been mounted on a blue folded card, which picks up the blue glow on the pear.

Ornate Trees

A simple tree stamp has been stamped in a row and coloured with horizontal bands of Perfect Pearls™, then decorated with holographic peel-off stickers. The middle tree was stamped first in order to achieve accurate spacing between the others. Once the trees had been created, the pearlescent ground was added using the textured sponge stippler from the main project. The black panel was torn and the edges given the same pearlescent treatment before being mounted onto gold card. The edge of the gold card was also torn to create a white border. This colour scheme offers a novel alternative to the traditional red and green.

Blossom Tags

The flowers were embossed on black card with a clear embossing powder. Colour has been added using Perfect Pearls™, mixed with water to create a paint medium. By painting on both sides of the embossed line, the image is brought to life. Three tags have then been punched from the painted flowers. Japanese paper cord and beads are used to embellish the tags – paper cord is easy to bend and to weave in and out of card. Glitter works well with pearlescent effects and is used here to highlight the flowers.

Collage

Collage is a French word that literally means to assemble and stick together. All kinds of items or images can be combined and composed into an arrangement that is pleasing to the eye. With stamping, images can be specifically crafted for the collage. The same stamp can be used to create a variety of collages, as it can be coloured, positioned and cut out in different ways.

In this stylish card – ideal for marking a number of occasions, such as retirement, moving abroad or a special holiday – a range of elements are successfully unified, either by colour or design. The colour wash technique is an easy, effective way of filling open areas of the design.

1 Using the fuchsia inkpad, stamp the French woman on a piece of cream linen card.

top tip

Apply a little extra pressure when stamping on linen or slightly textured card to compensate for the unevenness of the surface and to avoid losing parts of the print.

2 Using a wet paintbrush, drag out the colour from the stamped lines to fill some of the background areas. Also use the paintbrush to even out the colour in the solid stamped areas where you can see the grain of the linen card. Too much painting and the stamped images can disappear; too little and the washes look patchy. Once dry, trim the card around the border of the image.

3 Using the purple inkpad, stamp the 'bon voyage' background on another piece of cream linen card. Repeat the painting process used in Step 2 just over the 'bon voyage' words.

4 Make sure that the colour wash has dried before highlighting the words 'bon voyage' with black pen. If the card is taking time to dry, use a heat gun to speed up the process. If the black highlights are added while the card is still wet, they could bleed into the colour wash.

5 Turn the tag punch upside down. Slip the bon voyage-stamped card into the punch. Move it around until the words 'bon voyage' are positioned within the opening. Punch out the tag. Using the hole punch, make a hole in the top of the tag.

6 Place the French woman-stamped card and the tag on a piece of scrap paper. Using a Sponge Dauber™, pick up some ink from the orange inkpad and gently sponge over both items. Keep to the edges on the tag, but apply colour over the open areas of the picture.

7 Using the black inkpad, stamp the manuscript background on a piece of pale pink vellum. Allow the ink to dry before tearing away the edges.

top tip

Be careful when tearing vellum, as it seems to tear easily in one direction and unpredictably. Although this adds to the effect, you can be taken by surprise when it happens!

8 Fix an eyelet in the hole in the tag (see Step 9, page 112) and thread string through the eyelet. Gather together all the other items, including the buttons, and arrange on the cream folded card. Try out several layouts before stamping the 'par avion' and cancellation postmarks in a suitable gap. Stamp using the fuchsia and black inkpads respectively. Use the colour wash technique with the fuchsia ink on the 'par avion' postmark.

SMART STAMPING
Collage

✔ Pick a topic or colour theme to make it easier to collect and group items together.

✔ Select items that vary in size, texture and finish. Keep on the lookout for interesting items for collage, such as buttons, postage stamps, photos and labels.

✔ Raise some of the items in the arrangement to add spatial interest.

✔ Photocopy or scan any precious items so that you can cut them up and trim them as you wish. There are many vintage-style découpage materials for sale in craft shops. You can also age items such as paper with washes of cold tea and coffee.

✔ Stamps often come in ranges of designs, which means that you can select several stamps from a single range that will work together.

✔ Try out several layouts before securing the items.

9 Secure the vellum to the folded card using an eyelet in each of two opposite corners. Using spray glue, mount the main picture item onto the vellum and card. Place sticky fixers on the back of the tag to raise it. Use PVA glue to attach the buttons.

More ideas for collage

In the Pink

This design shows how a more structured approach can be used for collage. The white folded card has been stamped with a random pattern of safety pins. All the other elements were then created or gathered and arranged in a square formation, with the baby's handprint and vertical strip of images, created using a section of a paint swatch strip, providing the main definition of the shape. The baby bottle and tile demonstrate how successfully scrapbooking embellishments can be used for stamped cards. This design could be personalized for a special baby.

Oriental Lady

The oriental theme continues to be popular with stampers, so there is a good range of stamps, background papers and embellishments available in most craft shops. The oriental lady image takes centre stage on this card, with stamped motifs also used to create the additional tag and lantern elements. The vellum panel has been sponged and then stamped with Chinese characters, and the background papers selected to co-ordinate. The bead and flower are secured together with paper cord to add to the oriental theme.

Butterfly Collection

A colour theme of blues and pinks unifies the various stamped and printed paper elements here. As in the main project, all the items were stamped, coloured in, cut out or torn before being arranged on the folded card. The collage is in three layers – the first, items stamped directly onto the folded card and the sponging; the second, the items that have been stuck flat on the card, such as the vellum, butterfly tile and torn paper patches, and the third, items that are raised with sticky fixers, such as the daisy tag, cut-out butterfly and tiny metal butterfly.

Velvet Paper

You Will Need

- purple velvet paper
- gold card
- lilac velvet paper
- gold folded card 16.5 x 9cm (6½ x 3½ in)
- VersaMark™ or Clear Emboss™ inkpad
- flower stamp
- gold tinsel embossing powder
- iron
- Northwest corner punch
- gold thread
- lilac sheer ribbon

1 Using the clear inkpad, stamp the flower onto a piece of purple velvet paper 10.5 x 4.5cm (4¼ x 1¾in). Press down on the stamp with strong, even pressure to achieve a good print on the pile. Sprinkle the gold tinsel embossing powder all over the stamped flower.

Velvet paper mimics the qualities of the fabric perfectly. You can either stamp and emboss on the surface of the paper or use an iron to make a dry print into the pile of the paper, where the heat and pressure crush it against the stamp.

This sumptuous design has been embossed with gold tinsel powder – tinsel glitter powders cling more easily to the velvet surface. Gold thread wrapped around the panel makes an elegant frame.

top tip

Choose simple images without too much detail for stamping on velvet paper; the glitter may not adhere if the lines of the design are too fine.

2 Gently shake off the excess powder. The powder tends to cling to velvet paper, so you need to tap firmly on the back to encourage the stray specks to come off. Gently blowing over the image may also help. Return the spare embossing powder to its container.

3 If any unwanted specks remain, use a paintbrush to remove them. Removing the specks may take a little time and patience, but it is worth persevering to achieve a good finish.

top tip

Before using the iron, make sure there is no water in the steam compartment. The heat from the iron will not damage the rubber die.

4 Warm up the iron to the silk setting. Decide which areas around the flower are going to be dry printed. Turn the velvet paper panel over. Place the first selected area over the upturned stamp and press down with the tip of the iron over the back of the velvet paper. Repeat on the other areas. Be careful not to stamp onto the embossed flower.

5 Using spray glue, mount the panel on a slightly larger piece of gold card. Using the corner punch, punch two notches either side of the four corners of the gold card.

Velvet Paper 95

6 Using a small piece of adhesive tape, secure the end of a length of gold thread to the back of the gold card near one of the notches. Bring the thread round to the front of the card, making sure it is running through the notch. Continue to wrap the thread around the card using the other notches to keep the thread in place and to create a frame.

7 You should finish wrapping the thread where you started. Using a small piece of adhesive tape, secure the thread to the back of the card. Trim off any excess so that no loose ends will show when the panel is mounted on the folded card.

try this

For a quicker alternative, stamp the image onto velvet paper using a pearlescent Brilliance™ inkpad and colour in using colouring pencils or brush markers. Choose white or cream velvet paper for easy colouring.

8 Cut a piece of lilac velvet paper 16 x 8.5cm (6¼ x 3¼in). Using the same flower stamp, repeat the ironing process in Step 4 to dry print a random pattern all over the lilac paper. Mount centrally onto the gold folded card. Use glue strong enough to take the weight of the velvet paper, such as spray glue, or use double-sided tape.

9 Using sticky fixers, mount the embossed flower panel towards the top of the card front. Wrap a length of ribbon vertically around the left-hand side of the card front and tie in a bow.

More ideas for velvet paper

Glittering Bouquet

The bouquet has been stamped using a clear inkpad as in the project, but embossed with a silver glitter powder. Colouring pencils that co-ordinate with the velvet paper have been used to add the shading and detail. Although the surface of the velvet paper is textured, it is relatively smooth and even, and it will hold the colour from the pencil. The bouquet panel has been mounted on a square card, and to balance the composition, three flowers punched from velvet paper have been used to create a vertical border. Gems act as flower centres, adding to the opulence of the effect.

Christmas Nativity

This simple stained glass image of the nativity lends itself very well to being stamped and embossed on velvet paper. The same inkpad and powder have been used as in the project. Once the image had been stamped and embossed, the burgundy velvet paper was trimmed down using deckle-edged scissors. The panel was then mounted on gold card and the edges torn. Gold metal eyelets add decorative detail to the corners of the stamped panel. The base card has been covered with printed Christmas paper. Stars punched from gold card are positioned on the background to highlight the nativity panel.

Little Purple Number

The dress has been stamped and embossed as in the project, and colouring pencils used to add shading and detail, which brings a three-dimensional effect to the image. The stamped image itself has dots and circles, which have been used as a guide for positioning purple Diamond Dots™ along the embossed lines. Cross-hatching drawn with a white pencil breaks up the open background behind the dress. The completed panel has been mounted on layers of dark purple velvet and gold, with sheer ribbon underlining the overall impression of glamour.

Shrink Plastic

It is fascinating to watch shrink plastic twisting as it gradually reduces in size, and the end results enable you to produce quirky, scaled-down designs. The technique is a little challenging, in that the shrink plastic can react unpredictably, and you need a steady hand for stamping on the smooth surface.

Here, traditional festive colours combine with a contemporary-style shrink plastic tile. Sponging on the ink is a fast, easy method and has a softening effect.

1 Using the green inkpad, stamp the noel sampler onto the pre-sanded side of a piece of shrink plastic slightly larger than the image. Stamp carefully, avoiding any undue movement. Allow the ink to dry before handling. You can quicken the process with a heat gun, but do not get too close or the plastic will start to shrink!

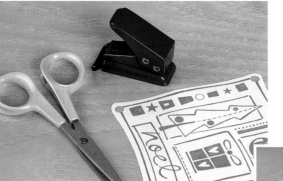

2 Cut out the sampler, leaving a small border around the image. A slightly uneven border will work best, especially as shrink plastic sometimes distorts during heating. Using the ¼ in hole punch, make a hole in each corner.

3 Place the piece of shrink plastic on scrap paper. Using a Sponge Dauber™, apply green ink to the surface of the shrink plastic. Try to vary the intensity of the sponging to create interest, allowing some of the areas of the white background to show through.

top tip

Always make any holes in the shrink plastic prior to shrinking and larger than normal, because it becomes thicker and brittle, and the holes will also shrink, when the plastic is heated.

4 Turn the piece of shrink plastic over and dust the back with a very small amount of talcum powder. The talcum powder will stop the edges of the plastic from sticking to each other as it curls and twists during the heating process.

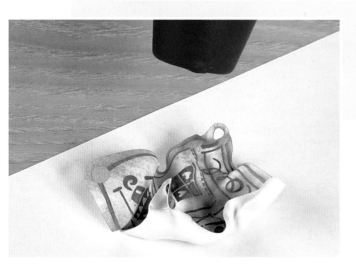

5 Using a heat gun, heat the shrink plastic, holding the heat gun about 2.5cm (1in) away and moving it around continually to heat it evenly. The plastic will curl and twist, but this is quite normal. Keep heating it until it uncurls and flattens. You may need to heat it from the back as well as from the front. Alternatively, put the shrink plastic onto a baking tray covered with foil and heat it in the oven according to the manufacturer's instructions.

6 To make the plastic completely flat, use a clean wooden block to press down on the back of the plastic on a clean surface. Make sure the plastic is still warm and flexible when you do this. Do not attempt this if the plastic is still curled up.

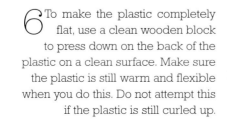

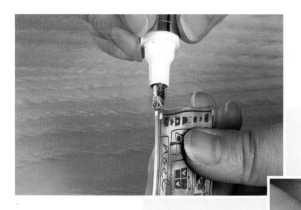

7 Holding the plastic tile in your hand, run the tip of the gold leaf pen around the edge. This has a wide chisel tip, which makes it easy to press against the side of the tile. Although barely visible, the gold tidies up the side of the tile and acts as a frame.

top tip

If you want to predict the exact amount of shrinkage, cut a strip of shrink plastic and draw a line on it. Measure and mark on centimetres or inches. Heat to shrink the strip and compare the new measurements to the original.

8 Tear a piece of red card about 6cm (2³/₈in) square. Use a piece of double-sided tape to secure the tile centrally to the red card. Using the ¹/₆in hole punch and the existing holes in the tile, punch four holes through the red card. Squeeze the punch just sufficiently to make the holes but not to damage the tile. Make four additional holes on the outside of the tile opposite the inside ones. Loop the wire several times through the holes on each corner. Finish with both ends of the wire at the back of the card and flatten down to secure.

try this

Use patterned papers applied to card, such as the one here, to make decorative backdrops for other card designs. It needs to be very lightweight, so that it won't tear along the spine when the card is folded.

9 Spray glue over the back of the white folded card. Place it centrally, glue-side down, onto a slightly larger piece of patterned paper. Trim off the excess paper. Using sticky fixers, mount the tile panel towards the top of the card and the gold heart beneath it.

SMART STAMPING

Shrink Plastic

✔ Use inkpads that are permanent or stamp with ink that will become permanent once it is heated. Brilliance™, ColorBox Fluid Chalks™, Fabrico™ and StazOn™ are all suitable.

✔ Bear in mind that colours intensify as the plastic is heated and shrinks.

✔ Pencils, chalks and acrylic paints can all be used to colour shrink plastic.

✔ The oven method of heating the shrink plastic is preferable for larger pieces, since the heat is more ambient.

✔ While still hot and flexible, the plastic can be moulded into different shapes, but be careful not to burn your fingers.

More ideas for shrink plastic

Giraffe Duo

See what a different effect can be achieved when the same giraffe image as used on page 57 is given the shrink-plastic treatment. Cream shrink plastic works well with the creams, browns and blacks used to stamp the giraffes. Several holes were punched along the side and bottom edges of the cut-out stamped panel before being shrunk. Once shrunk, the edges were sponged with brown ink. Wire was then wound through the holes in a spring shape, with beads added along the way. The central panel is framed by a hand-drawn stitched line, eyelets and a single button.

Frog Garden

The frog image was stamped in black on shrink plastic and allowed to dry before being filled in with colouring pencils. Once completed, the panel was cut out, leaving a narrow border on three sides and a slightly wider bottom border to allow for a row of punched holes. Heat was then applied to shrink the panel, intensifying the colours. Three tags were punched from a second stamped image, coloured in as the main image and a hole punched through the top before being heat shrunk. Wire is used to hang them from the frog panel, and plastic mosaic tiles embellish the background.

Dragonfly Paradise

The same stamp used to create the background was applied to a white shrink plastic square and tag before being shrunk. While the same multicoloured inkpad was used for both the background and the shrink plastic elements, the colours on the latter have intensified in the shrinking process, which makes them stand out. Before being heat shrunk, two identical dragonflies of different sizes were also stamped on the tag and square in contrasting black. Flowers punched from co-ordinating pearlescent paper add extra detail.

Metal Foil

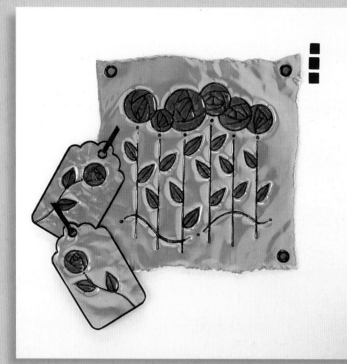

You Will Need

- ✿ green lightweight metal foil
- ✿ white linen folded card 14.5cm (5¾in) square
- ✿ jet black Staz On™ inkpad
- ✿ rose garden and single rose stamps
- ✿ foam mat
- ✿ dual dry embossing tool
- ✿ deep pink and green OHP (overhead-projector) pens
- ✿ peel-off stickers: black outline tags and eyelets, lines, squares
- ✿ ⅛in 'anywhere' hole punch
- ✿ 4 black ⅛in eyelets
- ✿ eyelet mat, setter and hammer

Stamping on metal foil, with its non-porous surface, requires a permanent ink, such as the StazOn™ inkpad used here, and its smoothness demands a controlled stamping technique. Any movement once the stamp is in contact with the foil will cause the image to blur, so the minimum amount of pressure is needed. OHP (overhead-projector) pens are ideal for using on metal foil – as well as being permanent, the ink is translucent, admitting the light that reflects off the foil's surface.

This Art Nouveau-style stamp design is influenced by the work of Charles Rennie Mackintosh, the Scottish architect, designer and painter, and stained glass windows. The vibrant jewel-like colours of the roses provide a perfect contrast to the metal foil.

1 Using the black inkpad, stamp the rose garden on a square piece of foil larger than the image to allow for tearing and two single roses on pieces slightly larger than the peel-off sticker tags. The ink will dry within 3–5 minutes of stamping, but a heat gun can quicken the process.

2 Place the foil on the foam mat and, using the fine ball on the dry embossing tool, draw directly onto the metal. Draw a broken line around the flower heads and leaves. Make sure that the broken line is on the outside of the stamped line and not directly on top. This will emphasize the design.

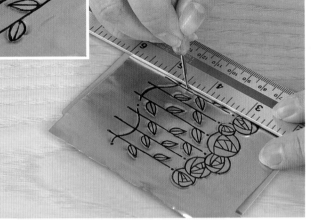

3 Using a ruler and the embossing tool, draw straight broken lines down the sides of the stems.

top tip

When drawing a continuous line into a foil surface, the metal can sometimes buckle up or concertina as it is pushed along, so by using a broken line, bumps and notches can be avoided.

4 Using OHP pens, colour in the flower heads and leaves. On the flower heads, colour from the centre outwards, as this avoids any buckling. As the foil is quite soft, the pens will push it down, adding to the effect.

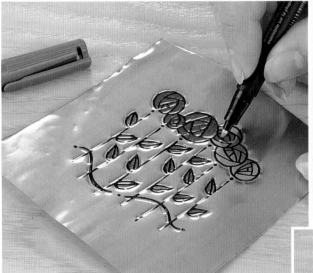

5 Tear away some of the background around the rose garden – the foil is soft enough to tear by hand. If you experience any difficulty starting to tear, make a small cut with scissors. Alternatively, use fancy-edged scissors.

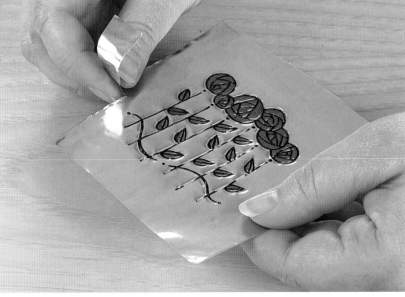

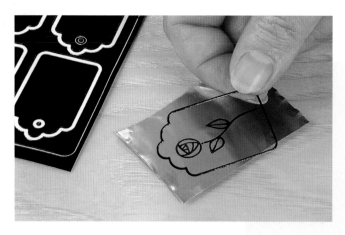

7 Using the hole punch, make a hole in the top of both tags. Position an eyelet from the tag sticker sheet over each hole. Cut out both tags. Handle the tags with care, as the metal foil is soft and bendable. As in Step 2, draw into the foil to highlight the flower heads and leaves, adding colour with the OHP pens. Make a tie for each tag with a peel-off line.

6 Lift a peel-off outline tag from the sheet and let it spring back to shape. Hover above one of the single roses to select the chosen area for the tag. Place the sticker in position and repeat the process for the second tag.

try this

To add further interest to a design, draw small circles all over the background to create a hammered metal-type textured effect.

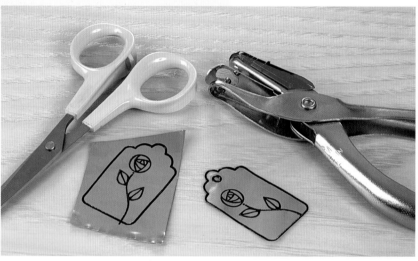

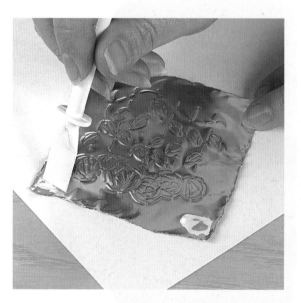

8 Turn the rose garden panel over and spread some PVA glue on the corners of the foil. Although the glue will take a while to dry, it is flexible and strong enough to stop the foil from lifting off. Mount the foil slightly towards the top of the white folded card.

SMART STAMPING
Metal Foil

✔ Metal foil comes in different thicknesses, so always check the packaging. Thicker foil, although more sturdy, is not so easy for drawing into. Lightweight foil is thin enough to punch, cut with scissors (straight- or fancy-edged) and tear.

✔ The lighter the colour foil, the easier it is to use for this technique. Gold and silver are the easiest to colour in.

✔ Bear in mind, when choosing colours to colour in the foil, that OHP pens, being translucent, will 'react' with the particular colour of the foil. Therefore, different shades will be produced than the original pen colour.

9 Using the hole punch, punch a hole in each corner of the foil panel and fix an eyelet in each (see Step 9, page 112). Place three little squares as an accent on the right-hand side of the foil panel. Using PVA glue, stick one of the tags overlapping the left-hand edge of the foil panel. Using sticky fixers, mount the second tag below and overlapping the first tag.

More ideas
for metal foil

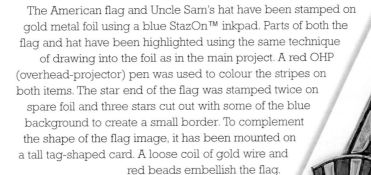

Celebrate USA

The American flag and Uncle Sam's hat have been stamped on gold metal foil using a blue StazOn™ inkpad. Parts of both the flag and hat have been highlighted using the same technique of drawing into the foil as in the main project. A red OHP (overhead-projector) pen was used to colour the stripes on both items. The star end of the flag was stamped twice on spare foil and three stars cut out with some of the blue background to create a small border. To complement the shape of the flag image, it has been mounted on a tall tag-shaped card. A loose coil of gold wire and red beads embellish the flag.

Say it With Flowers

This simple stamp of a decorated tag is ideal to use with metal foil. The flowers have an open design, which is simple to draw around with the dry embossing tool. Not all the tag is coloured in with the OHP (overhead-projector) pens, to allow the green metal foil to act as part of the background. The image has been stamped a second time so that sections can be cut out and used in the design. Small daisies have been punched out and added to the arrangement. Interesting eyelets in the shape of flowers and squares are used to dress the punched daisies and hole in the top of the tag. A wire loop replaces the traditional tag string.

Oriental Hanging

Although the stamp used to create this card is large, it prints up easily on the metal foil because of its fine lines and simple motifs. The whole panel has been used in this instance, but you could create a variety of cards by separating the squares into different groupings. The colours of the OHP (overhead-projector) pens work well with the oriental theme. The metal foil was thin enough for the panel to be cut out with deckle-edged scissors. Two small kebab sticks have been used to mimic poles so that the panel looks like a hanging, secured with thin wire to complete the effect.

Brayering

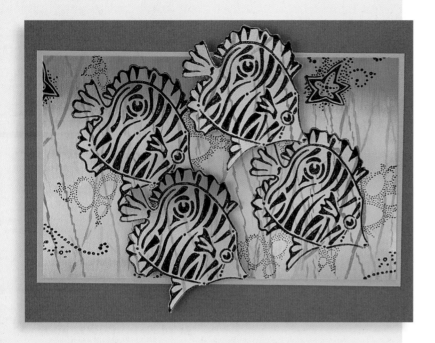

Amazing backgrounds can be quickly created by using a brayer and a multicoloured inkpad. And with a huge range of these 'rainbow' inkpads on offer, not only in intense tones but in soft, muted shades as well, you can select just the right range of colours to suit your chosen theme or occasion. Using a brayer is similar to handling a decorating paint roller – it must be evenly inked and applied.

The colours in this underwater scene mimic the effect of light shining through the depths of a coral reef. The technique of wrapping elastic bands around the brayer is perfect for creating the seaweed, but it would also work for grass or party streamers.

1 The inkpad used in this project is a multicoloured dye-based one. To avoid the inks running and mixing into each other, the bands of colour are divided into individual mini inkpads, which are stored apart when the inkpad is not being used.

top tip

Some multicoloured dye-based inkpads come as one large pad. These must be stored level and always the right way up.

2 Make these mini pads slide together by pushing the notch. Remember to slide them apart when not in use – the lid will not fit properly back onto the pad if you forget.

3 Anchor the pad down with your spare hand and ink up the brayer by rolling back and forth over the surface of the inkpad. Keep spinning it around when it is off the pad so that it is evenly covered. Roll it ever so slightly from side to side to lose the defined colour bands.

4 Put a sheet of scrap paper down on a large, flat surface. Place one piece of glossy card in the centre of the paper. Roll the brayer back and forth over the surface of the card, keeping to the same tracks. Press down hard and work quickly. Keep rolling until a good coverage is achieved. You will need to roll over the card several times and you may need to re-load the brayer.

top tip

If the colours that need to overlap are not compatible, then turn the card clockwise 180 degrees so that the same two colours will go over each other.

5 If the card is wider than the brayer, repeat Step 4. Re-roll over the edge of the last colour band to create a small overlap. Repeat the whole process with the second piece of glossy card.

6 Clean up the brayer and detach the roller from the handle. Wrap several elastic bands tightly around the roller along its length.

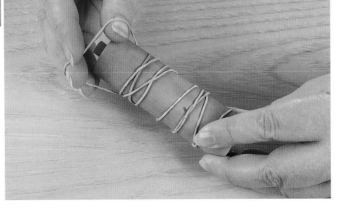

7 Ink up the elastic bands on the brayer. Although some ink will land on the roller, try not to press too hard on the inkpad. Gently roll the brayer a few times over one of the inked card panels from side to side in the opposite direction to the colour bands. Re-load the brayer and repeat with the second card panel.

8 Using the black inkpad, stamp two fishes on the first card panel and two fishes and several stars/starfish on the second card panel. Since the second panel will become the background, be careful where you stamp the fish. The stars need to be stamped over the edge of the panel.

9 Using small, sharp scissors, cut out the two fishes from the first panel. You may need to use a craft knife around the tails, working over a cutting mat. Using spray glue, mount the second panel onto a slightly larger piece of lime green card and then onto the front of the folded card. Add the two fishes using sticky fixers to complete the card.

try this

Ink up a textured surface with a brayer and take a print directly from the surface using bubble wrap.

SMART STAMPING

Brayering

✔ Brayering is easier on glossy card because the surface is coated and the ink has better coverage and goes further. Matt card can be used, but it is better for small items.

✔ Although most inks can be brayered, you must use a dye-based inkpad on glossy card.

✔ Try wrapping clingfilm and string around the roller as an alternative to elastic bands.

✔ Use a VersaMark™ inkpad to stamp onto glossy card before brayering the ink, which will act as a resist. As you brayer over the card, the images will appear as if by magic!

More ideas for brayering

Beaded Daisies

The multicoloured inkpad used for the brayering on this card is called Spectrum and is made up of very bright colours. However, as the inks blend together on the edges where they meet when brayered, the full impact of the colours is softened. A stamp with a textural design that mimics etched lines has been used to stamp the resist pattern for the background. The daisy trio has been stamped several times, with one whole trio used as the focus of the design, and the others découpaged and raised from the card surface with sticky fixers. Some of the daisy flower heads have been decorated with seed beads.

Baby Bear

A small bear has been stamped with a VersaMark™ inkpad to create a resist on some of the glossy card used for the background, then brayered with pastel-coloured inks, to emphasize the baby theme. The ink from this pad will stop any colour brayered over the top from reaching the card surface, hence the white outline. The large bear has been stamped with a black Brilliance™ inkpad on brayered card so that the gradation of colours is in the opposite arrangement to the background. Spare card was used for decorative punched-out flower shapes. Sticky fixers raise the main bear image and flowers from the background for added focus.

Aloha, Aloha

The sunset colours brayered on this card are perfect for the Hawaiian theme. A subtly patterned background has been created using the resist technique with a VersaMark™ inkpad and a large stamp comprising images of postage stamps. Spare brayered card was used for the stamped shirts and flip-flops, and for the punched-out flowers, which were backed with black card to cover the open holes. The surfboards were stamped on the background, which was then layered onto black card. Plastic shell beads add the finishing touch.

Acetate

top tip

When stamping a group of images in a row, stamp the central image first, then the other images either side, to make it easier to judge an even positioning within the available space.

The smooth, non-porous surface of acetate requires a special ink that will dry permanently, and without being heat fixed if the acetate is the kind that cannot be heated, such as the StazOn™ inkpad used here. Careful stamping is needed, as any movement once the stamp is in contact with the acetate will blur the image. Minimal pressure is also crucial, to avoid the stamp skidding on the slippery surface.

A swag of swinging baubles, stamped on an acetate strip, feature jazzy colours embellished with glitter. The transparent quality of the acetate is exploited by layering it over a background of stamped dots. Foil could be used as an alternative backing.

You Will Need

- acetate 7 x 17cm (2¾ x 6¾in)
- white linen folded card 8 x 17cm (3¼ x 6¾in)
- jet black StazOn™ inkpad
- bauble and large, medium and small dot stamps
- flexible ruler
- fine black, yellow, orange and magenta OHP (overhead-projector) pens or permanent markers
- Diamond Dots™
- yellow glitter
- yellow, orange and magenta pigment inkpads
- ⅛in hole punch
- eyelet mat, setter and hammer
- 4 gold ⅛in eyelets
- magenta sheer ribbon

1 Using the black inkpad, stamp three baubles along the middle of the acetate. Change the angle of the stamp each time to create the impression that the baubles are swinging. Be careful not to apply too much pressure on the stamp to avoid skidding. Allow the ink to dry for at least 5 minutes.

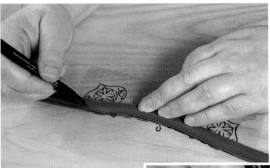

2 Check that the ink is thoroughly dry, then bend the flexible ruler into a gently curved line that will link up the baubles. Using a fine black OHP pen, draw a broken line against the ruler between the baubles.

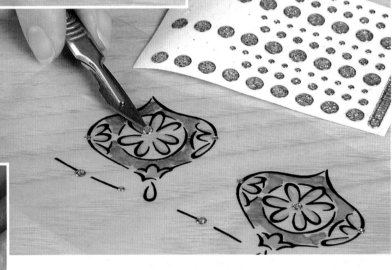

3 Using OHP pens or permanent markers, colour in each bauble in the same way with the three colours, leaving some areas uncoloured to create a more contemporary, 'arty' effect.

4 Using a craft knife, position Diamond Dots™ on the baubles and in the breaks in the hanging line. Use different-sized dots to add variety.

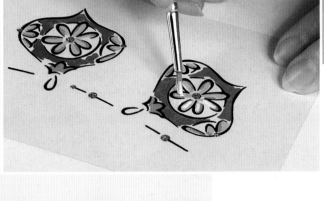

5 Using a fine paintbrush, apply a little PVA glue to each bauble at a time, highlighting the petals of the central flowers. Wash the brush thoroughly after use.

6 Sprinkle glitter over each flower. Tip off the excess glitter onto scrap paper. Fold the paper carefully and tip the glitter back into the jar. Allow the glue to dry thoroughly before handling the acetate.

7 Stamp dots in a band at random across the front of the white folded card. Using the yellow inkpad, start with the largest dot, leaving plenty of gaps in between. Stamp the medium dot next in orange – some of these dots can overlap the yellow ones. Finally, stamp the small dot in magenta. If necessary, you can go back and add extra yellow and orange dots.

8 Open the white folded card out flat, right-side up, on the eyelet mat. Position the acetate strip centrally on the front of the card over the band of dots. Using the hole punch, make a hole in each corner of the acetate and through the front of the card. Hold the acetate firmly in place so that it does not slip.

9 Push an eyelet through one of the holes in the acetate and the card. Turn the card over, holding the eyelet in place so that it does not fall out. Take the setting tool and place over the eyelet. Hit the top of the setting tool with the hammer. This will round off the back of the eyelet. Repeat the process with the other three holes and eyelets.

10 Turn the card right-side up again. Using the hole punch, make a hole in the hanging line either side of the hanging loop of the central bauble. Place the setting tool firmly over each hole in turn and hit the top with the hammer. Thread a length of ribbon through the holes and tie in a bow.

top tip

As acetate is transparent, you cannot use glue or double-sided tape to mount it on card. Eyelets are an ideal solution, but you could use corner slits, in which you can tuck the acetate corners. Special punches are available for making these.

More ideas for acetate

Fourth of July

Here, acetate has been used to layer over the blue card section of the background and for the main image panel, which is layered over white card. To achieve the colours of the American flag, the stamp for the main image was inked up using a red and a blue StazOn™ inkpad. Different-sized rectangles of blue and red card have been cut and combined to form a square, which has then been mounted on a white folded card. Wooden stars, the Class A Peels™ awareness ribbon and letter tile stickers have been added, and silver snaps decorate the opposite corners of the main panel and blue card section.

Shop 'til You Drop

This grinning girl has been stamped onto acetate using a black StazOn™ inkpad and coloured in using OHP (overhead-projector) pens. The acetate has been trimmed and mounted onto a slightly larger piece of yellow card, stamped with a subtle sixties-style 'flower power' pattern to create an appropriate background. All the colours featured on the girl's clothes and shoes are echoed in the buttons, snaps and card used for layering and mounting. This card would be great for a shopaholic or a sixties fan.

Hearts Galore

For this card, two large tags were cut, one from acetate and the other from white card. The hearts were stamped on the acetate tag using a red StazOn™ inkpad, while a matching dye-based inkpad was used to stamp the hearts on the white tag, which were then painted in using watered-down ink from the pad. The tags are tied together with sheer ribbon. Mini metal heart tags, embellished with matching sheer ribbon and wire, have been attached to the acetate tag using sticky fixers. This would make a cutting-edge wedding invitation.

Style Stones

Style stones are versatile embellishments made from cultured stone. Available in a range of useful shapes, including tags and hearts, their flat surfaces are ideal for stamping and sponging. They can be used as the focal point of a card design or as a decorative element.

In this project, the tag-shaped style stones have been stamped with a section of the large stamp to create a different yet co-ordinating pattern. Simple wire and beadwork has been used with the tags to give an extra, contemporary dimension to the design.

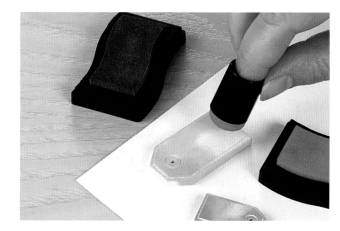

1 Using a Sponge Dauber™, dab the tags with ink, applying the ink with variable pressure to achieve a mottled finish. Start with a layer of the lighter mandarin ink and allow to dry before adding the darker henna colour. Use a heat gun to quicken the drying process between the layers. Handle the tags as little as possible, as the ink will lift off while it is still wet.

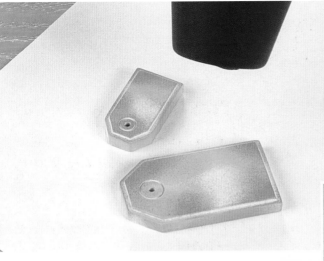

2 When the sponging is completed, use the heat gun to fix the ink. The heating process will make the ink layers permanent on the tags. Allow the tags to cool down completely before handling, as they will get quite hot.

3 Study the collage image carefully and decide which part of the design you want to use. Remove the brown block from the Crafter's™ inkpad and ink up your chosen section of the stamp. Press the stamp down gently on one of the tags. Re-ink the stamp and repeat for the second tag. Heat the tags with the heat gun to fix the ink.

4 When the tags are completely cool, use the copper leaf pen to edge the recesses of the tag edges with colour. The flat nib of the pen makes it easy to run along the edge. Allow the copper to dry before handling.

5 Cut a rectangle of cream linen card 7.5 x 6.5cm (3 x 2½in). Using the mandarin and henna inks, sponge the card in the same way as the tags. As the inks are quick to dry, a mottled effect is easily achieved.

6 Using the brown Crafter's™ ink, stamp the collage image onto the sponged card.

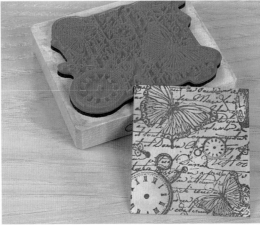

7 Using the brown Crafter's™ ink, stamp three butterflies down the right-hand side of the cream linen folded card. Stamp one of the butterflies over the edge of the card to make an interesting arrangement. Dry the butterflies with the heat gun. Press both the mandarin and henna inkpads against a piece of foil to make a simple paint palette. Using a wet paintbrush, pick up the paint from the foil and apply to the butterflies.

top tip

When picking up the paint from the foil palette, add more or less water to vary the intensity of the colour. When the colour runs out, revive with another print from the inkpad.

8 Place a piece of torn scrap paper over the front panel of the folded card, covering the left-hand side of the butterflies. Sponge mandarin ink over the edge of the torn paper across the area of the card left uncovered. Sponge over the butterflies. Repeat the process on the left-hand side of the card.

9 Using spray glue, mount the stamped collage panel on the left-hand side of the folded card. Using the hole punch, make a hole in each corner of the panel and fix a snap in each hole, using the same method as for eyelets (see Step 9, page 112). Thread a length of copper wire through each tag. Keep the ends of the wire together with a bead. Using a cocktail stick, curl the ends of the wire into a coil. Use adhesive dots to secure the tags to the card.

SMART STAMPING
Style Stones

✔ Style stones are available in two finishes, coated and natural.

✔ The stones that are coated are ivory coloured and have a flat surface ideal for stamping and sponging.

✔ The stones that are natural have an engraved surface. Simple stamped patterns and sponging work best with these stones.

✔ Use permanent inks to stamp and sponge onto the stones.

More ideas for style stones

Little Acorns

The maple leaf recess on this style stone was coloured in using light-coloured ink, applied with a sponge. Dark brown ink was then added to the flat surface before it was stamped using a small acorn stamp. A similar stamp design was used to create the random leaf pattern on the card. The corrugated card, wooden beads and raffia reflect the nature theme of this card. The style stone is glued to the card, the wire in this instance being purely decorative.

Rose Panel

Three smaller stones linked together with beads and wire create the main focus of this design. The stones were sponged with pink and purple inks before being stamped with the same rose stamp used for the background, with black ink creating contrast. The bleaching technique was employed to achieve the background. The roses were stamped on purple card using black ink, then bleach was used to lighten areas of the flowers and background. The stones were wired together before being stuck to the card.

Celtic Blues

The style stone on this card has a recessed Celtic design engraved in its surface. Blue ink was sponged into the recess before the actual surface was coloured and stamped on. The blue folded card was sponged with a darker tone of ink to create a criss-cross pattern. Celtic stamps were then used to stamp the central panel and torn strips. The Celtic patterns on all these pieces have been embossed with a green pearlescent powder. Thin wire, doubled up and threaded with beads, attaches the style stone to the card.

Suppliers

The author would like to thank the following suppliers for providing copyrighted images and/or products to enable her to produce this book.

UK

F W Bramwell & Co Ltd
Old Empress Mills
Empress Street
Colne
Lancs BB8 9HU
tel: 01282 860388
fax: 01282 860389
email: info@bramwellcrafts.co.uk
www.bramwellcrafts.co.uk

Hobby Art
23 Holmethorpe Avenue
Holmethorpe Industrial Estate
Redhill
Surrey RH1 2NL
tel: 01737 789977
email: hobbyartstamps@fsmail.net

SLP Partners Ltd
23 West View
Chirk
Wrexham LL14 5HL
tel: 01691 774778
fax: 01691 774849
email: sales@slpuk.demon.co.uk

The Stamp Man
8a Craven Court
High Street
Skipton
North Yorkshire BD23 1DG
tel/fax: 01756 797048
email: TheStampManUK@aol.com
www.thestampman.co.uk

Woodware Craft Collection BV
Unit 2a
Sandylands Business Park
Skipton
North Yorkshire BD23 2DE
tel: 01756 700024
fax: 01756 701097
email: sales@woodware.co.uk

USA

Art Institute Glitter
720 N Balboa Street
Cottonwood
Arizona 86326
tel: toll free [877] 909-0805
email: info@artglitter.com
www.artglitter.com

Artistic Wire Ltd
1210 Harrison Avenue
La Grange Park
IL 60526
tel: 630-530-7567
fax: 630-530-7536
email: carilm@artisticwire.com
www.artisticwire.com

Clearsnap Inc
PO Box 98
Anacortes
WA 98221
tel: 360-293-6634
email: contact@clearsnap.com
www.clearsnap.com

D J Inkers
PO Box 467
Coalville
Utah 84017
tel: 800-325-4890
www.djinkers.com

EK Success
261 River Road
Clifton
NJ 07014
tel: 800-524-1349
fax: 973- 594-0540
email: sales@eksuccess.com
www.eksuccess.com

Emagination Crafts Inc
463 W Wrightwood Avenue
Elmhurst
IL 60126
tel: 630-833-9521
fax: 630-833-9751
email: service@emaginationcrafts.com
www.emaginationcrafts.com

Hero Arts Rubber Stamps Inc
1343 Powell Street
Emeryville
CA 94608
tel: 800-822-HERO
fax: 800-441-3632
email: info@heroarts.com
www.heroarts.com

Inkadinkado
61 Holton Street
Woburn
MA 01801
email: sales@inkadinkado.com
www.inkadinkado.com

Judikins
17803 S Harvard Boulevard
Gardena
CA 90248
tel: 310-515-1115
fax: 310-323-6619
email: customerservice@judikins.com
www.judikins.com

McGill Inc
131 East Praire Street
Marengo
IL 60152
tel: 815-568-7244
email: sales@mcgillinc.com
www.mcgillinc.com

Paper Adventures
901 South 5th Street
PO Box 04393
Milwaukee
WI 53204
tel: 800-727-0699
fax: 800-727-0268
email: cs@paperadventures.com
www.paperadventures.com

Penny Black Rubber Stamps Inc
PO Box 11496
Berkeley
CA 94712
tel: 510-849-1883
fax: 510-849-1887
email: sales@pennyblackinc.com
www.pennyblackinc.com

PSX
360 Sutton Place
Santa Rosa
CA 95407
tel: 707-588-8058
fax: 707-588-7476
email: info@psxdesign.com
www.psxdesign.com

Ranger Industries Inc
15 Park Road
Tinton Falls
NJ 07724
tel: 732-389-3535
fax: 732-389-1102
www.rangerink.com

Rubber Stampede Inc
2550 Pellissier Place
Whittier
CA 90601
tel: 562-695-7969
email: advisor@dtccorp.com
www.rubberstampede.com

Retailers

Stampendous Inc
1240 North Red Gum
Anaheim
CA 92806
tel: 714-688-0288
fax: 714-688-0297
email: stamp@stampendous.com
www.stampendous.com

Stewart Superior Corp
2050 Farallon Drive
San Leandro
CA 94577
tel: 510-346-9811
fax: 510-346-9822
email: sales@stewartsuperior.com
www.stewartsuperior.com

Tsukineko Inc
17640 NE 54th Street
Redmond
WA 98052
tel: 425-883-7733
fax: 425-883-7418
email: sales@tsukineko.com
www.tsukineko.com

Uchida of America Corp
3535 Del Amo Boulevard
Torrance
CA 90503
tel: 310-793-2200
fax: 800-229-7017
email: marvy@uchida.com
www.uchida.com

USArtQuest Inc
7800 Ann Arbor Road
Grass Lake
MI 49240
tel: 517-522-6225
fax: 517-522-6228
email: askanything@usartquest.com
www.usartquest.com

Canada
Magenta Rubber Stamps
2275 Bombardier Street
Sainte-Julie
Quebec J3H 3B4
tel: 450-922-5253
fax: 450-922-0053
email: info@magentastyle.com
www.magentarubberstamps.com

UK
Card Inspirations
The Old Dairy
Tewin Hill Farm
Tewin
Welwyn
Herts AL6 0LL
tel: 01438 717000
fax: 01438 717477
email: info@cardinspirations.biz
www.cardinspirations.co.uk

Centagraph
18 Station Parade
Harrogate
North Yorkshire HG1 1UE
tel: 01423 566327
fax: 01423 505486
email: info@centagraph.co.uk
www.centagraph.co.uk

The Craft Barn
9 East Grinstead Road
Lingfield
Surrey RH7 6EP
tel: 01342 832977
fax: 01342 836716
email: info@craftbarn.co.uk
www.craftbarn.co.uk

Craft Creations Ltd
4B Ingersoll House
Delamare Road
Cheshunt
Herts EN8 9HD
tel: 01992 781900
fax: 01992 634339
email: Enquiries@craftcreations.com
www.craftcreations.com

Craftwork Cards
Unit 2
The Moorings
Waterside Road
Stourton
Leeds
West Yorkshire LS10 1DG
tel: 01132 765713
fax: 01132 705986
www.craftworkcards.com

Dorrie Doodle
50 Bridge Street
Aberdeen AB11 6JN
tel/fax: 01224 212821
email: dorrie@dorriedoodle.com
www.dorriedoodle.com

Eclipse Cards and Crafts
Market Hall
Balcony Shop
4 Tennant Street
Derby DE1 2DB
tel: 01332 208308
fax: 08700 519195
email: info@eclipsecardcraft.co.uk
www.eclipsecardcraft.co.uk

LA Designs
25 High Street
Milford on Sea
Lymington
Hants SO41 0QF
tel/fax: 01590 644445
email: Lyn@LA-Designs.co.uk
www.LA-Designs.co.uk

Sirstampalot
Thurston House
80 Lincoln Road
Peterborough PE1 2SN
tel: 01733 554410
fax: 01733 554486
www.sirstampalot.co.uk

The Stamp Man
(See Suppliers for details)

Tonertex Foils Ltd
PO Box 3746
London N2 9ED
tel: 020 8444 1992
fax: 020 8883 0845
email: info@tonertex.com
www.tornertex.com

Product Details

Découpage (page 42)
Stamp: DeNami 118 Full-View Butterfly
Peel Off's™: AC623 Brads & Eyelets

Shadow Stamping (page 46)
Stamps: Hero Arts H2552 Six Irregular
Background Blocks, LL862 Artistic Hearts,
A2269 Small Open Block
Karisma™ colouring pencils: dark purple
and white

Chalks (page 50)
Stamps: Hero Arts LL874 Real High-
Country Wildflowers

Sponged Backgrounds (page 54)
Stamp: Stampendous P102 Sketched
Blossoms

Bleaching Out (page 58)
Stamps: Stampendous P056
Suzanne Bouquet, E157 Dragonfly
Stampendous Class A Peels™:
Flutterbies AC613G
Karisma™ colouring pencils

Embossing Pens (page 62)
Stamps: Hero Arts LL886 Autumn Harvest
Fancy Notes
Tsukineko Emboss Dual Pens™: Spring
Green, Emerald, Tangerine, Chocolate
Peel Off's™: AC623 Brads & Eyelets

Multi Embossing (page 66)
Stamps: Stampendous N030 Peacock
Feather, JudiKins 2422J Porcelain

Masking (page 70)
Stamps: Stampendous V033 Prancing
Zebra, Q099 Heart Drop Trio

Cut Away (page 74)
Stamps: PSX K-1911 Back to Back Bears,
SK606C Hug Me Teddy

3-D Découpage (page 78)
Stamp: Woodware Craft Collection
FRM002 Funky Tree
Peel Off's™: 91151 Funky Christmas
in Gold
Karisma™ colouring pencils

Vellum (page 82)
Stamp: Stampendous PO99 Dress Up
Peel Off's™: AC622 Flower Eyelets

Pearlescent Effects (page 86)
Stamp: Penny Black 2829K Brush Lily
Peel Off's™: AC623 Brads & Eyelets,
97802 Oriental 1, 92667 Bamboo Borders

Collage (page 90)
Stamps: Hero Arts G2812 Woman in
Profile, G2701 Bon Voyage Background,
H2141 Manuscript, A2194 Par Avion,
A2234 Luxe Cancellation

Velvet Paper (page 94)
Stamp: Woodware Craft Collection
FRN004 Tapestry Flower

Shrink Plastic (page 98)
Stamp: Woodware Craft Collection
FRW001 Noel Sampler

Metal Foil (page 102)
Stamps: Woodware Craft Collection
XXQ004 Glasgow Rose Garden and
XXB003 Glasgow Rose
Peel Off's™: 91958 Small Tags,
AC623 Brads & Eyelets, 91799 Lines,
91955 Random Tiles
Staedtler Lumocolor™ OHP pens

Brayering (page 106)
Stamps: Woodware Craft Collection
XXQ009 Barry Reef, Stampendous
L102 Stardust Points

Acetate (page 110)
Stamps: Hero Arts LL882 Heritage
Ornaments, LL909 Lots of Dots
Staedtler Lumocolor™ OHP pens

Style Stones (page 114)
Stamps: Inkadinkado 91034.X Time Flies
Collage, 90582.M Butterfly
Krylon™ copper leaf pen

About the Author

Françoise Read has been stamping for more than 12 years
and designing stamps for over 7 years. Françoise was
teaching arts and crafts at
secondary school level when she
first caught the rubber stamping
bug. She has designed stamps
for both British and American
companies, and is currently
in-house designer for Woodware
in the UK. Françoise's love of
designing has led her to use
her creative ideas to develop
collections of Peel Off's™
stickers, a range of background
papers as well as card embellishments. Françoise writes and
creates for various magazines, including *Crafts Beautiful* and
Practical Crafts. Françoise's work has been featured in several
other stamping books, including one of her own. Françoise
also runs stamping workshops for stampers and retailers,
and demonstrates regularly across the UK. She has a design
studio at her home in Berkshire, England, where she lives
with her husband Paul and son Liam.

Acknowledgments

A special thanks to the team who worked on my book,
especially Fiona, commissioning editor; Jennifer, editor; Lisa,
senior designer; Jo, project editor; and last but not least, Karl,
photographer, who was brilliant both with ideas and support.

This book was written during a very difficult period of time,
during which friends and family offered me the greatest
support, enabling me to complete this task. To all of them,
a special thank you: Mum and Dad, Linda, Sue, Kevin, Mark
and Barry.

To Judith of Woodware and Maggie for giving me the time,
space and support to write this book, thank you also.

Index